Russe
decad
and t
His p
Crime
Cross
Acid

FITTED UP

A TRUE STORY OF POLICE BETRAYAL CONSPIRACY AND COVER UP

RUSSELL FINDLAY

BIRLINN

First published in 2019 by
Birlinn Limited
West Newington House
10 Newington Road
Edinburgh
EH9 1QS

www.birlinn.co.uk

ISBN: 978 1 78027 539 0

British Library Cataloguing-in-Publication Data
A catalogue record for this book is available from the British Library

Typeset by Initial Typesetting Services, Edinburgh
Printed and bound by Clays Ltd, Elcograf, S.p.A.

Quis custodiet ipsos custodes?
(Who will guard the guards themselves?)

CONTENTS

Prologue

THE FIRE

Army veteran Bill Johnstone controlled the cold rage welling up inside his chest. He stood watching helplessly as his garage burned to the ground. Ferocious flames crackled in the November night air as oily black smoke swirled high above the frosted white rooftops of Glasgow's West End.

As the fire spread, police officers hammered on doors, pressed buzzers and barked urgent orders at scores of neighbouring residents to wake up and get out immediately. Confused and worried elderly householders and parents with sleepy children had no time to salvage possessions as they were evacuated from the warmth of their red sandstone tenements to the safety of nearby Hyndland Secondary school.

Bill stood with his partner, Jackie Mills, powerless to do anything other than mask his nostrils from the billowing, acrid stench. They shrank back from the blistering wall of heat and watched as the inferno's orange glow danced on the walls of the now empty flats and incinerated his business premises. The blue lights of fire engines added to the colourful display.

Bill was a well-known figure in the used car trade, buying and selling cars, and specialising in classic vehicles, which he picked up at auctions around the country. With a reputation as an honest broker, who had a keen eye for a bargain and an encyclopedic knowledge of rare and unusual vehicles, he had built Turnberry Motors from scratch in the 18 years since the end of his army service. Occupying a small corner of cobbled ground where Turnberry Road meets Hayburn Lane, wedged between a small park and the railway line that runs north-west from the centre of Glasgow, the garage was Bill's livelihood and he was proud of what he had achieved. Now, at the age of 52, Bill still carried the no-nonsense demeanour of a hardened military man. Lean, alert, serious and straight-talking, he was not the type of man to be taken for a fool.

As firefighters contained then extinguished the blaze, Bill told two uniformed female police officers about a heated dispute that had taken place seven months earlier in April, with a customer named John Lawson.

Bill told the police that Lawson had paid £150 for a clapped-out Ford Transit van which had no MOT and was sold as scrap, yet he had returned to the garage to complain about its condition and demanded compensation – £1,900 being the figure he deemed fair but which was patently nonsensical. With a bitter tang of alcohol on his breath, Lawson paid him two further visits and in front of several witnesses made noisy demands for this compensation. 'I'll tan your motors,' Lawson is accused of saying. 'I'll wait until you've got better ones in, cos they're not good enough. I'll burn down your garage.' At the time Lawson was dismissed as a harmless nuisance, told bluntly where to go, and he had slunk away empty-handed, muttering to himself. There had appeared to be little point in reporting such ravings to the police.

Had such an encounter occurred several years earlier, Lawson may not have been so lucky. In the years immediately after leaving the army, a younger Bill would have responded with more than expletives.

The pair of uniformed female officers listened and took Bill's details. They asked him to stay at the scene, as the CID would need to speak to him, but by 2 a.m. they had not arrived. A non-fatal fire was low priority when compared with the CID's standard Saturday night diet of drink-fuelled street crime. The officers told Bill that he could go home, with the assurance that detectives would contact him in the morning and that a forensic examination would take place.

Hesitant to leave the scene, Bill was convinced by the officers and Jackie that there was nothing he could do, that it would be better to get some sleep and come back the following morning.

When he and Jackie returned to the garage after a restless night, dawn's light revealed a skimpy line of fluttering blue and white police tape around a scene of scorched earth devastation – a shell of brickwork and steel; blackened and jagged windows and the skeletons of seven classic cars including an extremely rare 1960s Reliant Scimitar. It looked like a war zone or the site of a bomb blast, familiar scenes during Bill's military service.

Part of Bill wanted to take matters into his own hands, to go straight to the suspected root of his problem, but he was talked down by the common sense of Jackie, who persuaded him to do it right, to have faith in the system. He waited patiently all day on Sunday for the promised call from the CID but it did not materialise, no matter how hard or often he stared at his phone.

Patience is not one of Bill's strongest virtues.

Over the coming decade, his patience would be tested in the most extraordinary way. The fire at Turnberry Motors was just the beginning.

Four days after the fire – on Wednesday, 11 November – with ribbons of blue-and-white tape still dancing in the breeze, Bill had still heard nothing back from the police.

The blaze had started on the night of Saturday, 7 November 2009 and Bill had been assured CID officers would be in touch to take a statement. That having failed to happen, as Sunday passed and his anxiety rose, Bill determined to visit Partick police station himself. That evening he was introduced to DC Campbell Martin, a police officer who would figure on numerous occasions in Bill's fight for justice.

Bill had passed on a potentially useful lead – that some neighbouring residents had seen the blaze take hold on the railway embankment side of the garage premises. He asked DC Martin what was being done and pointed out that any slim chance of yielding forensic evidence from the site was diminishing with every passing hour.

The CID officer said the possible presence of asbestos was preventing the fire service from conducting their investigation of the site and that he was not prepared to take a statement, as his night shift colleagues would be dealing with it. Then came a phrase which Bill would become wearily familiar with over the coming weeks, months and years: *Someone will be in touch. Goodbye.*

But as the days passed, Jackie began to share Bill's growing astonishment that an incident which could have killed sleeping families in their beds and had destroyed their livelihoods was being treated with a lack of urgency. They couldn't fathom whether this was down to laziness or indifference. Perhaps because it had been commercial rather than residential premises, and no one was hurt, the police were simply not interested.

Having failed to get the attention of police officers by visiting Partick station, Bill asked Jackie if she would help. As the constituency office manager for SNP MSP Sandra White, and the election agent for another of the party's MSPs, Bill Kidd, Jackie sent an email to Chief Superintendent Anne McGuire, who was in charge of the local division. Jackie articulated Bill's frustration at being let down and pleaded for action to be taken.

The string-pulling had an immediate effect. The following day, 12 November, an inspector invited Bill to Partick, where he was to speak with him and DC Martin, who had turned him away four days earlier.

Even before the garage fire, Bill had little faith in the police. Some of his suspicion and cynicism was a legacy of serving in Northern Ireland during the bloodshed and terror of the 1970s and 1980s, where he witnessed serious injustice and corruption by some RUC police officers and even fellow soldiers.

Nonetheless, and although five days too late, he welcomed the opportunity to finally be able to provide police with a full and detailed account in the hope that it would jolt them into action and attempt to bring the fire starter to justice before any further attacks could took place.

In the statement, Bill went back over the minutiae of the van dispute and again provided details of those who had witnessed John Lawson's alleged threats. Bill also told of two other acts of vandalism in the month before the fire when a vehicle transporter's tyres had been slashed and the windows of a Mercedes car smashed. These had not been reported at the time because Bill had considered it pointless. Only now did he realise they may have been committed by the same hand as the fire.

In addition he told Martin that another mechanic who worked from a nearby unit had suffered a similar alleged threat from Lawson in a row over who was liable to pay a parking ticket. The mechanic and his colleague told Bill that Lawson had threatened to torch their unit unless they paid the ticket. This was a potentially crucial piece of information.

It turned out that Bill's low expectations were too optimistic. The asbestos at the garage site was of a type that
posed no health risk and did not require specialist removal
but no forensic examination ever took place. No CCTV
cameras in the surrounding area were ever checked. The
neighbours who had seen the fire take hold were never
spoken to. Door-to-door enquiries did not happen. The
mechanic who said that he had suffered a similar alleged
fire threat from Lawson heard nothing from the police.

Only five months later in April 2010 – after official complaints were logged by Bill – did officers make a cursory
attempt to speak to those who had made the 999 calls
about the blaze, although they still did not speak to the
witnesses who had told Bill they saw it begin.

Bill also discovered that the fire had not been categorised
as a crime in the police computer system, which meant he
was not given a reference number of the type assigned to
every alleged offence. Over the following years, the police
changed their official position in relation to the fire's
status. First there came the dismissive pronouncement
that there were 'no suspicious circumstances' – a wholly
unsustainable claim, given the complete failure to investigate. Then the police stated that they 'could not establish' if it was suspicious, an acceptance that their original
claim was untrue because they had not conducted any
investigation.

Their position later shifted again significantly to admit
'the cause of the fire was unknown', as fresh evidence
emerged that it *had* been deliberate.

But back in November 2009, with less than a week
having passed since Turnberry Motors was razed to the
ground, Bill and Jackie were only beginning to realise
they were on their own. What they did not appreciate was
that life would never be the same again. The garage fire
marked the beginning of an astonishing chain of events

that would consume their lives and put them under immense pressure for more than a decade, perhaps even longer.

The retired soldier would be dragged back into battle. At stake were his finances, freedom, health . . . even his life. It was a battle he did not seek and did not want, but his only choice was to fight or be destroyed. His foe was not just the fire starter, but also the police.

1

THE ARMY: SQUARE GO

'Who's Bill *fucking* Johnstone?'

So the fresh young recruits stepping from the bus at the British Army's Salamanca barracks in West Germany were welcomed. Asking the question was Ayrshire soldier Ricky Ferguson, who'd been tipped off that Johnstone might be a challenger to his title of Royal Artillery 16th Regiment bare-knuckle boxing champion.

Bill Johnstone exited the bus that frozen February morning in 1975 and made himself known with the snarled response, 'Who's *fucking* asking?'

Introductions over, Ferguson ordered him to be in the gym at 9 p.m. for a 'square go' but Bill – eschewing Queensberry Rules for the Gorbals' version – immediately lashed out with a ferocious blow to his rival's face, sparking a blur of fists. After several minutes of toe-to-toe combat in the snow and gravel, they were prised apart and handed cans of beer and cigarettes before a second round of intense pummelling began. The spectating soldiers' cheers and heckles were punctuated by the steady and soft thud of fists on flesh. Bruised, bloodied and blowing white plumes into the winter air, the exhausted pair was eventually separated and, with mutual respect, a draw was declared.

Born in Paisley before moving to Glasgow's Gorbals –
whose local hero was diminutive boxer Benny Lynch – Bill
later spent most of his childhood in the sprawling
Easterhouse estate, where his Catholic mum overruled
his Protestant dad to send their boy and four sisters to
the Catholic St Leonard's secondary school. As a 14 year
old who excelled at athletics and karate, he enrolled in
the Prince of Wales Sea Training school in Dover. With
pupils drawn from across the Commonwealth, the rough
young Glaswegian stood out and thrived, his ability to
learn and follow orders earning him the title of 'leading
boy' for the entire school, a prestigious position to hold.
For three years he travelled the world in giant container
ships and oil tankers. As 'engine room boy' he was tasked
with dangling by a rope on a bosun's chair into hot,
dark, cavernous oil storage tanks, where, with no safety
equipment and cloying chemical fumes penetrating the
senses, he'd blast a hydraulic gun against the hardened
crude oil encrusted to the sides. On board vessels such as
the 10,000-tonne MV *British Dragoon*, Bill would often not
see land for months, but he enjoyed the discipline and
adventures far from home.

While visiting family in Glasgow, and having just turned
17, life took a dramatic change of direction due to a chance
encounter in a city centre pub with Brian 'Woody' Woods,
an old school pal who was in the army. Resplendent in
naval uniform of bell bottom trousers, Bill was drinking
in the gloom and smoke of the Ingram Bar when Woody
spotted him. Having regaled the bar with his capers as a
member of the Royal Artillery, Woody then imparted to
Bill some considered career advice: 'Fuck that navy shite!'

Persuaded by his friend's wise words and action-packed
tales, the very next morning Bill joined up at the army
recruiting office in Queen Street, a few doors down from
the pub. Two weeks later he was on a train to the Royal

Artillery barracks at Woolwich, London. That first night, the stifled sobs of green recruits could be heard in the dorms, but Bill, having already travelled the world by sea, and imbued with discipline, slept soundly.

The initial intake of 200 dwindled steadily, with around 30 men left standing at the end of 26 weeks of basic training. Many of the drop-outs and rejects simply could not handle the harsh physical demands, spartan conditions and terrifying instructors, like the Irish NCO Sergeant Joe Fury, whose name matched the apoplexy of his orders. Fury had a fine line in nicknames for his charges, with Bill identified as 'Cunty McFuck'.

Just as Bill had stood out during his merchant navy training, his natural virtues of industry, discipline, intelligence, tenacity and fitness were recognised in the army, and he was named best gunnery student, another impressive accolade. Gunner Johnstone was then put on a bus to join the 16th Regiment in Germany, where he did not yet know that his 400-mile journey would end with Gunner Ferguson waiting for a scrap.

The 16th air defence regiment, while open to all British Army recruits, is unofficially known as the 'Glasgow Gunners' because of the large number of men from Scotland's most populous city within its rank, and it is renowned for being robust and efficient.

With the Cold War set to permafrost in the late 1970s, they were part of the NATO force primed and ready for a Russian attack. Much of their time in Germany's Rhine Valley was spent wearing cumbersome suits which were supposed to protect them from chemical and biological attacks or the aftermath of a doomsday nuclear strike from the Kremlin. If the Cold War had turned hot, the official lifespan of these 'forward edge of battle area' soldiers was two hours, which was probably optimistic. They would likely have been vaporised in a heartbeat.

Bill became part of a four-man specialist reconnais-sance unit whose job it was to get as close as possible to enemy positions and set up OPs (observation posts), where they would remain entrenched, the eyes and ears of the regiment, undetected for weeks on end. Resilience and physical endurance were key attributes. Patience was learned with difficulty.

While off-duty, these disciplined but hardened young men didn't need much encouragement to unwind. Bill and a friend once drunkenly attempted to sneak two German girls into the barracks in the back of a taxi, only for their amorous plot to be thwarted by Gordon Highlanders on guard duty.

Having been caught, Bill's pal inflamed the situation by questioning the sexuality of the kilted soldiers who had spoiled their fun: *weren't they the Gay Gordons?* Goading escalated into a punch-up. The Gordons were sober and more numerous, so there was only ever one outcome. Bill and his pal put up a decent show but were given a sound hiding.

When they awoke in the cells nursing bruises and sharp hangovers, they were marched in front of the Gordon Highlanders' regimental sergeant major, who locked them up for seven days. This being military justice, a second judge awaited. The 16th Regiment's regimental sergeant major gave them another seven days to be served consecutively. Part of their punishment was to paint the base's seemingly endless miles of kerb-stones black and white. For hours on end they worked, the monochrome pattern burnished on to their brains even when their eyes were closed for sleep. This incident was enough to blot Bill's otherwise untarnished record and prevented him from receiving the medal which is awarded to military personnel for long service and good conduct. It takes just one black mark to stop this medal from being pinned on a soldier's chest, no matter how exemplary his entire service.

Bill quickly learned that soldiers did what they were told and had no rights. Any thought of complaining – let alone being granted a fair hearing – was fanciful. One regimental sergeant major's office door displayed a witty and ironic sign, stating 'RSM and complaints department'. If any NCO or officer wanted to discipline a soldier, he could come up with any reason to do so. Evidence was not necessary. All they needed was Section 69. This catch-all regulation could be applied to just about any misdeed, real or perceived. For example, if a solider sincerely attempted to answer a question screamed in his face, this in itself could be classed as insubordination – a Section 69. If they kept their mouth shut, then it was 'silent insubordination' – also a Section 69. This contradictory dilemma was a classic double bind, as made famous by the satirical Second World War novel *Catch-22*, which military veterans recognise all too well.

Military courts-martial were ridiculously one-sided and could hear dozens of cases in a day. Bewildered soldiers would be marched in, almost always found guilty – and then asked if they would accept the consequent 'award'. It was a rhetorical question. The senior officer acting as judge would only then reveal the punishment.

Bill honed his bare-knuckle pugilism by sparring with travellers on gypsy camp sites in Scotland and was so skilled at various martial arts and unarmed combat that he started instructing other soldiers how best to break bones up close. One day he and Joe McDermott, a fellow Glaswegian and member of 16th Regiment who became a lifelong friend, were at a large tented army camp in the village of Sennelager, an hour east of Salamanca barracks. As the two men were practising their skills with nunchucks – Japanese martial arts sticks – they were met with wolf whistles and jeers from a watching gaggle of bored English soldiers of a light infantry regiment. Without hesitation, the two men put down their sticks, unsheathed their long and sharp trench bayonets, and marched over to the English camp, where they spat out the offer of a 'square go' to any of the 'fucking comedians' present. The sight of two approaching savages, waving bayonets though massively outnumbered, immediately silenced the mocking. Their tormentors raised their hands, broke eye contact and melted away, mumbling, 'Only joking, Jock. No need to be like that, no one wants any trouble'.

Even for the Glasgow Gunners, Bill was at the extreme end of the spectrum. Aged 19, he was as lean, powerful and quick as a professional boxer but with the added element of having a cold and obedient military mindset, of being capable of killing and wounding without pause for thought. He was ferocious. These traits saw him thrive in the army, but they would also serve him well many years later when faced with enemies in Scotland – people who should have been on his side.

2

THE RAZOR BLADE

By the beginning of December 2009, with his vehicles destroyed in the garage blaze, Bill took off for London to attend a classic car auction, hoping to restock his business. It was as much to do with getting out of town as any serious buying, as there could be no quick fix to the financial disaster wreaked by the fire. He and Jackie were ostensibly away on business but they also needed some breathing space, time to clear their heads and assess events back home.

Jackie's elderly father, Jack Mills, was looking after the couple's post during their absence, piling up incoming mail on the kitchen table of their comfortable detached home in the West End of the city. Amongst the bundle of bills, marketing junk and glossy leaflets for takeaway pizzas was a white envelope containing a nasty surprise.

As they sifted through the mail on their return, Jackie handed the envelope to Bill. It was addressed to him, although she commented on the handwritten scrawl, which was like that of a pre-school child. When Bill tentatively opened it, another white envelope – cut in half – fell onto the table. Inside the half envelope was a doubled-edged razor blade, the thin steel glinting in the kitchen light. The postmark date was 30 November. Presumably the sender's intent was to inflict fear – or a nasty finger cut. For a man like Bill, it was as childish a threat as the writing on the envelope. The message was crude, and may have seemed laughable, but Bill was smart enough to understand that, after the fire, it had to be taken seriously – the cowardly sender knew where he lived, and who knew what he was capable of.

Bill and Jackie put the items into a plastic bag, which they took to the police station the following morning, 9 December, passing the evidence to DC Vicky Reid for the attention of DC Campbell Martin.

Just as before, Bill and Jackie were sent away: *Someone will be in touch. Goodbye.*

The next day they heard nothing from the police, but Bill picked up whispers from a car trade contact that John Lawson had been visited by DC Martin on 29 November and that he had not been happy about the attention – although he was apparently cocksure enough to think he had nothing to worry about. The envelope's postmark therefore meant something: the razor had been posted the day after Lawson's police visit.

At around 11 p.m. on 11 December, Bill finally managed to get DC Martin on the phone and could barely believe what he was told. The detective informed him that the fire case had been closed due to lack of evidence. The police had singularly failed to investigate the fire, but had now closed the book on it because they had not found any evidence. It felt like a police take on a military catch-22.

In relation to the razor blade, Bill was told that it could take up to a *year* to have it forensically examined. Martin also told him that Lawson had provided an alibi for the night of the fire and he believed it to be plausible. Bill's military experience had instilled in him the discipline to maintain his cool in circumstances which would cause others to become emotional. This time, he came close to losing it.

He bridled at not only what Martin was telling him but also the high-handed, dismissive tone in which it was delivered, with jarring phrases such as 'end of story' and 'case closed' sounding like provocation.

Trying hard to contain his fury, Bill addressed the young detective. 'Son, you have done fuck-all about the fire or the blade, be under no illusion that you're not walking away from this.' Before the officer could respond, Bill cut him off. 'My granny would make a better fucking detective than you,' he snarled at him.

The heated phone call was suddenly terminated and when Bill immediately called back to continue his unsolicited appraisal of Martin's detective skills he was told by another officer that he was no longer available.

Bill was seething. His £300,000 garage and £80,000 collection of cars had been destroyed. He had received a razor blade at his home. He was concerned that the vendetta would escalate. Most of all he was worried about the well-being of his family, not least his three younger children to his former partner. Yet the police – making a mockery of their oft-stated 'Keeping People Safe' PR mantra – were either disinterested or being plain lazy.

Bill turned to his lawyer, Chris Rogers, who from his office in Rutherglen sent a letter to the police complaints and discipline unit. His letter, faxed on 16 December, set the tone for much of the future correspondence:

> Our client [Bill] heard, through a third party, that the suspect [Lawson] had been interviewed on 29 November but nothing further was to happen. DC Martin did not advise our client of this. Our client received in the Royal Mail a letter posted on 30 November, the day after the suspect had been interviewed. This item contained a razor blade. The item was handed to a police

station on 9 December (our client had returned
from London on 8 December) for the attention
of DC Martin. He was promised a return call on
9 December. No call was received. Our client
telephoned DC Martin on 11 December. He was
advised that the case 'had been closed due to
lack of evidence'. He was further advised that it
could take 'up to a year' to have the postal item
forensically examined.

Our client is utterly vexed that there has been
minimal investigation into his concerns. No witnesses have been interviewed; there has been no
attempt to establish the cause of the fire.

Our client now has genuine fears for his own
safety and for the safety of members of his
family. He feels that there has been a complete
lack of regard for his complaints here and that
further, more serious incidents may take place.
He alleges that the suspect is a dangerous and
bizarre individual. We await your confirmation
that these matters will now receive the appropriate attention to the satisfaction of our client.

Whenever the public reports a matter to the police, an
incident number is automatically generated. It is up to
the police to then decide whether or not an incident
should be categorised as a crime, thereby generating a
crime report which carries a unique reference number.

The crime reference number allows any police officer
who has any involvement in the case to add updates to
the computer system, creating a chronological account of
what action has been taken, the identity of the officer who
took it and the exact time they did so.

Many years later Bill made the startling discovery that

when he handed the blade to police the case was not allocated an incident number. There was no good reason why this was not done at the time. It was not until 9 a.m. on 17 December – eight days after he gave the blade to police and, more tellingly, the day after his lawyer's fax landed at police HQ – that Martin got round to raising an incident number. Then, just one hour after finally raising the incident number, Martin logged an update on the crime report for the fire, requesting that he should also be allocated the blade inquiry on the basis of his knowledge of the incident.

The crime report further reveals an apparently reasonable suggestion from Martin that the blade inquiry should be put on hold until forensic analysis took place. 'The envelope and razor blade will be submitted for forensic and fingerprint examination,' he wrote in his report. The only problem was that no forensic analysis was ever ordered.

This extraordinary document raised serious and worrying questions. But Bill knew none of this at the time – it would be *six years* before he would discover these astonishing entries in the crime report, and then due only to his single-minded tenacity.

A lot was going to happen in those six long years.

3

VENDETTA

Ugly white grooves had been cut deep into the blood-red paintwork of the sleek Alfa Romeo GT parked outside the home of Bill and Jackie. Someone had sneaked along the sleeping street in the dead of night and, applying heavy pressure with a sharp blade, left their crude marks on the glossy metal. The jagged lines were carved into every single panel of the beautiful Italian coupé. The targeted and deliberate attack was not the type of inconvenient little scrape inflicted in a supermarket car park. Bill would have to pay out £2,000 to repair the damage.

It had been four months since Turnberry Motors was destroyed and three months since Bill received a razor blade in the post and, as he had feared and articulated to the police, his tormentor did not seem to be interested in going away.

The purpose of the cowardly act of vandalism was to create fear. The depth of the scratches suggested they had been made with something more substantial than a key or penknife, meaning the perpetrator may have been confident enough to wander the dark street with a blade.

Most unsettling was the realisation that they had been watched. The Alfa belonged to a friend and Bill had parked it on the street outside his house only two days earlier. The only way anyone would know of its connection to Bill was if they had seen him driving it.

In the weeks previous to this, there had been other incidents, of Jackie or Bill answering their mobile to an anonymous caller who had stayed silent on the end of the line. Jackie is quieter than Bill, but her outward reticence should not be mistaken for weakness. She possesses qualities of quiet and steadfast determination, a willingness to plough on without fuss and not to be fobbed off. So, jolted by the attack on the Alfa, she went to Partick police station that same day to voice mounting concerns to DI William Park. Not only did she feel personally under threat and vulnerable, she was also worried sick about her 82-year-old father Jack Mills and 15-year-old schoolboy son, who shared their home. The pressure on Jackie was beginning to mount.

When uniformed police officers turned up the day after Bill reported the Alfa Romeo incident, on the morning of 15 March 2010, he retold his story to them from the beginning.

When Bill left the house three days later, on the morning of 18 March, the nightcrawler had again been at work and another message was waiting. A Mercedes SLK320, which belonged to Jackie, had received similar, albeit less extensive attention from a blade, with thick scores carved along an entire side of the car's silver paintwork. Again, two uniformed officers attended and were told the ever-lengthening story anew.

Giving statements to the police, insulting the police, getting angry with the police, complaining to the police and pleading with the police had achieved little – other than the absolute failure of the police to conduct any meaningful acts of policing.

With no other options available, for the second time Bill sought the assistance of his solicitor, who in the months after the garage fire had composed the powerful letter of complaint.

A second letter was dispatched by Chris Rogers on the same day that the damaged Mercedes was found. He wrote: 'It does not appear that any proper investigation of these incidents [garage fire, razor blade, car vandalism] has taken place. None of the witnesses concerned have been interviewed (persons who heard the threat to burn down the garage).'

And in a stark warning that the vendetta could escalate to an altogether more serious level involving serious injury or death, he added:

> It remains only a matter of time before further, more serious, incidents occur unless proper police attention is taken to matters. The criminality here is likely to take the suspect [John Lawson] to a High Court indictment. The frustration and anger of our client [Bill Johnstone] ought to be fully understood by the police.

Even though the letter caused no discernible change to police conduct, it served as a useful record of events, charting each incident and each failing.

Meanwhile, work had been done to clear the debris of the garage fire. The classic cars' skeletons were removed from their crematorium and what was left of the unstable structure was demolished, yielding around 100 bags of rubble, timber, steel and glass, which sat on the site ready to be taken to landfill.

Almost three weeks after the vandalised Alfa Romeo and Mercedes, Bill was driving towards the site along Turnberry Road when he suddenly saw a familiar figure. Head down, walking quickly away from the garage down Hayburn Lane, it looked like John Lawson. Despite living in relatively close proximity, their paths rarely crossed.

Bill suppressed the urge to leap from his car and take direct and effective action, knowing that his own arrest would follow the satisfaction of physically harming Lawson. As he stopped at the garage, the first thing he noticed was a gushing sound. A jet of water was shooting into the air and creating a rapidly spreading pool of water.

A water hose lying on the site had been cut and a high-pressure jet arced upwards. Dozens of the bulging rubble bags had been ripped open, sliced apart with a blade, the contents spilling out like entrails.

Bill grabbed his phone and called the direct number he had been given for the CID office in Partick police station and explained the urgency of the situation. He stayed on the line and turned his car back down Turnberry Road, then took a left into Dudley Drive, which took him onto Clarence Drive and gave him a brief glimpse of the suspected perpetrator disappearing out of sight under a railway bridge. The police warned him to forget any notion of pursuit.

Bill ended the call and returned to the garage, where he followed the cut hose to a metal pipe protruding from the concrete floor. Using a brick, with cold water blasting into his face and body, he managed to hammer a bend into the metal pipe, stemming but not stopping the incredible flow pouring onto the lane.

Soaked to the skin, he sat in his car with heaters on full blast, windows misted, waiting for police to arrive. The call to the CID was made at 9.45 p.m. on the night of 5 April, but it was past 11 p.m. before two uniformed officers rolled up to the garage, where they were met by a soggy man with steam rising from his clothes, if not out of his ears.

He explained that upon arriving earlier in the evening – to swap the car he was in for another which he was taking to auction – he spotted the furtive figure he thought was Lawson walking away. He then retold his entire story, starting with the £150 van dispute one year earlier.

The following day CID officer DS Monica Haddock and her colleague met Bill at the site and listened again to the background before taking away the length of cut hose in an evidence bag with an assurance that it would be forensically tested.

Unbeknown to Bill at the time, just like the posted razor blade, no testing was ever instructed. Many years later, criminal advocate Paul Nelson became involved in Bill's saga. Nelson, a former Crown Office prosecutor who held a diploma in forensic medicine, was nonplussed at the police decision not to test the evidence.

In an opinion note produced by Nelson in 2014, he wrote:

> I am disquieted to note that the absence of forensic examination of this pipe is due to it being covered 'in dirt and oil and is considerable in length, due to this and the nature of this crime it is not suitable for forensic examination'. I am unconvinced by the logic of that statement.

On 8 April, Bill and Jackie were called back into Partick, where they were taken into a tiny, grimy room almost entirely filled by a small table and four chairs, two on each side. Waiting for them was DS Haddock and old sparring partner DC Campbell Martin.

Bill wanted to know what telecommunication checks were being done in relation to the silent calls he and Jackie were getting and if there was any progress in relation to the other crimes, not least the most recent one of cut pipe and rubble bags. This little chat did not go so well.

Jackie took exception at DC Martin's continued asser-
tion, initially made almost five months earlier, that it
could take a year for forensic tests to be carried out on
the razor blade and envelope. DC Martin qualified this
by saying that it could be 'up to' a year. The subtlety of
the disputed position made no difference, as it amounted
to the same thing. That niggle was one of many where
Bill and Jackie's expectations and beliefs that enquiries
were being made, tests conducted, CCTV checked and
witnesses traced turned out to be wishful thinking.

Jackie is usually slower to anger than Bill, but as she sat
in the stuffy little box, the clever attempts at evasion and
wordplay caused her to lose her temper.

'I've had enough of this shite,' she snapped. She then
looked directly at Martin. 'And by the way, you will *not* be
shrugging us off. We want answers.'

She rose sharply to her feet and headed for the door,
slamming it behind her and walking out to the bus fumes
and bustle of Dumbarton Road. Had she not left, she was
sure such was her fury that she could have reached across
and struck Martin, whose startled appearance suggested
he was unused to being spoken to in such a manner.

Bill believed that the police had decided to do as
little as possible about the spate of crimes because of their
initial failure to properly investigate the garage fire. To
properly pursue investigations into the later crimes would
not only draw attention to the fire failures but also raise
awkward questions about why they had occurred and who
was responsible.

Or as Bill puts it: 'They were not interested in going
after Lawson because they'd fucked up over the fire. The
problem was they had no idea how far this would go.'

It is not difficult for the police to downplay events. A
£400,000 garage fire is wrongly described as 'non suspicious' and not even recorded as a crime. No one is hurt,

why should they care? A posted razor blade is allocated an incident number only after a lawyer complains – and is then given the relatively petty tag of 'breach of the peace'. Cars trashed by a blade-wielding maniac become mere 'vandalism' in the crime stats. A deliberate flood, caused by someone using a knife, is just a cut hose pipe – who cares?

The police did not want to join the dots, to link the growing list of crimes. In isolation, many of them could be recorded and treated as fairly trivial, but when put together the picture that emerges is incredibly ugly.

The truth is that police officers did nothing to protect an innocent, hard-working family as their lives were being ripped apart in a sustained and sinister criminal campaign at the hands of someone who had no intention, apparently, of stopping. Its longevity denied logic – but since when did every act of criminality need to make sense? For all anyone knew, this person may also have been capable of damaging *people* beyond repair.

On Dumbarton Road, Jackie stood shaking with rage and blinking back angry tears as she tried to comprehend why the police were feeding them nonsense and treating them like fools. A few minutes later she was joined outside by Bill.

It was time to go home.

4

THE ARMY:
DERRY WELCOME

The transition from Cold War games in icy eastern European forests to the white-hot bedlam of urban Northern Ireland was a remarkably easy one for the teenage solider from Glasgow.

Bill was part of a small Royal Artillery advance party which joined the Royal Green Jackets regiment as they liaised to hand over the British Army base in the heart of Londonderry, or Derry, as most locals know it.

It was 1976 and Northern Ireland was in an abyss of violence and terror which would ultimately claim the lives of around 3,600 men, women and children.

Bill had spent three months in Sennelager, where the Ministry of Defence recreated typical Northern Ireland streets and buildings, complete with dummies of women pushing prams and other everyday scenes. No matter how convincing the dioramas and realistic the training in Germany, nothing could adequately prepare soldiers for the utter madness and mayhem that awaited.

During the six-month tour, Bill experienced murders, bombings, snipers, riots and the ever-present risk of sudden and violent death. It was an extreme environment in which he thrived. He was just 19 years old.

A company of the Glasgow Gunners was based in the fortified car park of the Masonic Hall in Bishop's Gate, one of the four original portals around the seventeenth-century city walls. It was a makeshift camp, mostly open to the elements and constructed from rudimentary wooden cabins. One day Bill was standing naked and shaving when a bullet pierced the ceiling and shattered the white porcelain sink right in front of him. He was unscathed other than a mere nick from the razor blade. This near miss was officially classed as possible sniper fire . . . truth was, it was a 'negligent discharge' by a hapless soldier.

In those early years of the Troubles, the epicentre was Derry, specifically the Republican and working-class strongholds of Bogside and Creggan, which effectively became no-go areas for the Royal Ulster Constabulary police force, whose officers were mainly Protestants.

Each British Army foot patrol was comprised of eight men, known as a section. A section was made up of two four-man groups known as a 'brick'. Each brick had two pairs of soldiers, whose job was to watch each other's backs – known as a 'Buddy-buddy'.

Bill's back was covered by Joe McDermott, with whom he had challenged English soldiers for mocking their nunchuck practice. In Bill's words, he and Joe were 'game as fuck', which was useful because patrolling Bogside and Creggan in British Army uniform was to paint a target on your back. Joe was Catholic, while Bill, who was half-Catholic, albeit with no interest in religion, shared the disdain for the bigotry which hung heavy in the air. They were as thick as thieves. Joe was a model soldier with nerves of steel and a cool head. He was the ultimate 'Buddy-buddy'. As far as they were concerned, any bastard who tried to kill them was their enemy and they would act the same way towards Republican or Loyalist thugs with weapons.

A few weeks into the tour, the reality of their circumstances hit hard. As their section tentatively fanned through Bogside, the radio crackled the code denoting one of their own was down. Lying dead with a sniper's bullet in his head was William 'Buff' Miller, aged 19, who was the first and youngest Royal Artillery fatality of the Troubles.

By the time Bill's section jogged to the nearby scene, large numbers of locals were pouring out from flats, houses and around every corner. The soldier's murder had become a clarion call to riot.

With no time to mourn, the Glasgow Gunners raced to the barracks to change into protective body armour and helmets with visors, then return to Bogside.

The *Derry Journal* recorded what happened under the headline 'DERRY'S WORST DAY OF VIOLENCE FOR YEARS', with a list of the destruction that had followed:

> ... a 19-year-old British soldier killed by a sniper; business premises in the city centre either destroyed or badly damaged by bomb explosions which were followed by fires; a hotel blasted in another bomb explosion; and rioting. This was the catalogue of death and destruction of one of the worst days of violence Derry has experienced for some years.
>
> The young soldier who died was Gunner William Miller, of the 16th Light Air Defence Regiment, Royal Artillery. He was on sentry duty at Butcher Gate pedestrian checkpoint when shot in the head by a sniper.

Miller was not forgotten. On the 40th anniversary in 2016, ex-comrades and family members paid their respects at the young man's grave in Larkhall, Lanarkshire. No one was ever brought to justice for his murder, although intelligence later suggested that the likely perpetrator was a

Swedish mercenary who learned his sniping skills while with France's Foreign Legion before joining the IRA as a hired gun, a theory only now being made public.

The ensuing riot lasted long into the night. Such outbreaks became common, with soldiers often spending up to 18 hours dodging bricks, bottles, bullets and petrol bombs. Some of the hate-filled mob tried to blind them by spraying toxic liquid through viewing slits of Humber Pig armoured vehicles. One soldier whose face was permanently maimed by an acid bomb became nicknamed 'Beetroot', typical of the army's brutally dark humour.

Bill and his comrades were no more than boys when they were thrown into this maelstrom, which was both physically draining and mentally exhausting. The soldiers' senses were amplified by pure adrenaline – acutely aware that one small mistake, or simply bad luck, could put them back over the Irish Sea in a body bag, just like their pal Buff.

None of the young squaddies were short on bravado. Some were reckless, bordering on insane. One 16th Regiment lance bombardier accepted a bet to go for a pint in an IRA-controlled pub right beside the 'Free Derry' gable end mural in Bogside. He somehow got away with it and collected his winnings.

Bill's section was in Creggan beside a gas works when it discovered a suspicious box with a cable running from it buried into the ground. Bill gulped with trepidation when his section commander Sergeant Robert 'Scrumpy' Hall ordered him and Gunner Tony Calpin to go and take a look. Seeing that it was indeed a shoe box with a cable coming from it, he deployed a rudimentary but useful piece of kit – a metal hook on a length of string. Attaching the hook, he took cover and yanked off the lid, but there was no explosion.

The section commander – at a safe distance and protected by a brick wall – then ordered Bill to go and have

another look. After all, they didn't want to call out the
bomb disposal boys for nothing.

Bill edged slowly back to see wires and a detonator. He was
lucky. Had the bomb gone off beside the gas storage tanks,
he would have been turned to ash. Another possibility was
that the bomb was a sniper's lure. It was a common tactic
of the IRA to set an explosion which would draw British
soldiers into the crosshairs of a hidden sharpshooter.

When Bill recounted his actions to the bomb disposal
experts, they simply shook their heads and chuckled at the
gung-ho recklessness of the Glasgow Gunners. Looking
back, Bill can only laugh at the naivety of his actions but
concedes that he had no choice but to follow orders.

While patrolling Bogside, Gunner Robert 'Rab'
Ferguson was shot through the hip by a sniper – the
high-velocity round spinning his metal water bottle 200
feet down the street. A split second earlier he had been
crouching beside a car. Had he not risen, the bullet would
have penetrated his skull.

The shot came from the notorious Rossville Flats, which
four years earlier had been the scene of Bloody Sunday,
where 13 unarmed civil rights protestors had been killed
by British Army Paras. The hatred towards the army was visceral. Bloody Sunday became a focal point of Republican
anger and undoubtedly fuelled rather than subdued the
violence as the Paras seemed to think it would.

By the time Bill and his section arrived at the high-rise,
some members of Fergie's section had gone inside to
search every flat from the top down, while others dragged
the injured soldiers out of the firing line. Bill and Joe
went the opposite way, from bottom to top, systematically
forcing residents' doors in the hunt for the sniper. They
stopped when their radios told them that *two* of the
enemy were dead. The army's subsequent official enquiry
accepted the questionable account that one sniper fell

out a window while trying to escape and the other had jumped to his death rather than be captured. In the fog of war, a dirty war, little scrutiny was applied to many such deaths and Bill would never know the truth of what happened that day.

Death became near normal. During a routine foot patrol, they discovered the fetid corpse of a suspected IRA man, his feet sticking out of a large wheelie bin. The bullet hole in his forehead suggested execution for being a suspected informant. The rats had already feasted on his eyes, brains and guts.

Bill and his comrades were more concerned that the body was a trap to lure them into a sniper's sights, so they worked quickly to throw it into a Land Rover and dump it unceremoniously at the morgue. The mortuary staff casually issued a receipt.

On another occasion, when a tip-off led them to the Bogside home of an IRA quartermaster, they did not expect to find anything significant, so were delighted at the cache of weapons and explosives stashed beneath floorboards and behind false walls.

What was then the largest arms haul in Bogside brought Bill to the attention of Grenadier Guards officer Captain Robert Nairac. Bill and Joe were manning a rooftop observation post in the city centre when Nairac stopped by with a bearded workman who was wearing overalls and carrying a tool box. However, he was no ordinary workman, but an intelligence officer whose toolbox contained a hidden camera. During the chance meeting, Nairac got chatting and told Bill and Joe that he had been impressed with the Bogside arms find.

Nairac was involved with a shadowy branch of the military that used covert intelligence and counter-insurgency techniques. The unit, whose name and personnel constantly shifted and evolved, was later accused of operating a 'shoot to kill' policy and colluding with Loyalist execution gangs.

Nairac seemed to suggest to Bill that there may be an opportunity to work alongside his men.

This apparent job interview was as opaque as the unit under Nairac's command but would propel Bill's career in a very different and even more dangerous direction, away from the streets and into the shadows. Any normal job interview which results in employment comes with a clear contract of employment. In 1980s Northern Ireland, while working in the shadows, such matters were not so simple. Often a soldier's status was not always clearly defined, allowing for fluidity and secrecy of movement. A year after their friendly chat, Nairac was captured, tortured and murdered by the IRA. His body has never been found.

Most of these raw young men had little knowledge of the history that had created the war in which they were fighting and had no real understanding of the factions involved. The IRA was clearly the enemy, but during that first tour Bill also began to question the role of the (now defunct) RUC. At best, he viewed the RUC as an irrelevance – it could not even enter parts of Derry where soldiers put their lives on the line every single day. While many very brave and decent RUC personnel were murdered during the Troubles, Bill also saw evidence of deep-seated religious bigotry within its predominately Protestant ranks. With a Catholic mum and Catholic schooling, he had zero tolerance of the mindless stupidity of religious hatred – whether back home in Glasgow or on the streets of Derry. Bill could see how the RUC's treatment of Catholic communities exacerbated the volatile situation and created even more violence, which the army then had to deal with. Bill's view of the police was shaped in the Bogside in 1976 and it never left him. In future years, his wariness would serve him well.

5

MISSING WITNESSES

John Lawson was a welder in his fifties who rented a lock-up close to Turnberry Motors and lived three miles away in the 1950s Cadder housing estate. He made a living picking up odd jobs in affluent West End enclaves such as Dowanhill, Kelvinside and Hyndland – the kind of places where the residents tended not to get their own hands grubby. He was not immune from the police. However, when they did take action against Lawson, Bill was puzzled by their plodding pace and curiously half-hearted reluctance, even resistance.

As the flames were still rising from his garage, Bill had told the uniformed officers on the ground about the £150 van dispute which culminated in Lawson's alleged threat to torch the business and cars. He had supplied names and contact details of witnesses then.

Bill was asked to give a formal statement about the threat incident, but he was only invited in after the email to Chief Superintendent Anne McGuire that Jackie sent in her role as an employee of MSP Sandra White. '[Bill] has been the victim of a crime in which he has lost his business,' her email had stated, 'and yet no one is investigating the suspicious circumstances or even contacting him to let him know what's happening. While it should not have taken her intervention to open the door to Bill, he had taken that opportunity to impart everything he knew on a formal basis.

His detailed account, given to DC Campbell Martin in Partick police station, ran to around a dozen A4 pages. Within it, Bill reported two distinctly separate issues – the garage fire and Lawson's alleged threat in April 2009. Little did Bill know that the police's apparent interest was just a charade. Smiles, handshakes and reassurances complete, they sat on Bill's information.

He had again provided the names and business addresses of witnesses. These people were all known to Bill and they were not difficult to find. But they were never traced.

It was more than two months after the fire, and after relentless calls and cajoling by Bill and his lawyer, that the alleged threat to burn down the garage was even given an incident number. This happened exactly one day after Bill's lawyer Chris Rogers phoned police HQ to demand proper action be taken.

But another two months were to pass before the police created a crime report.

The failure to give an incident number, let alone create a report, was an odd breach of protocol. The question was: what would motivate police officers to sit on their hands and ignore a crime? The explanation is unsavoury but makes perfect sense.

In the CID's immediate rush to wrongly dismiss the fire as 'not suspicious', the die had been cast. There was no requirement for the police to commit resources to investigate the incident. Ergo, there was no desire to speak to the witnesses who were present when Lawson allegedly imparted his fire-raising threat. To pursue them would have potentially risked giving credence to Bill's view that the fire was more than an accident or act of God.

The reluctant detectives, however, did not give enough consideration to one crucial factor: the type of character Bill is. He is not someone who waves a white flag. He is fastidious, bordering on obsessive, this being evident from the way he presents himself to the world and in his unshakable determination to challenge every single point of contention.

For months he chipped away at the police, demanding to know what was being done about the threat. He didn't want special treatment, just some basic policing. The officers he spoke to could not keep their fingers in their ears indefinitely . . . Or could they?

It took more than five months of perseverance to force a breakthrough, with Lawson being invited to voluntarily attend a city centre police station in April 2010, when he was interviewed by DC Vicky Reid and another officer. Lawson was charged with breach of the peace by threatening to set fire to the garage and vandalising cars one year earlier.

Bill and Jackie's relief and pleasure at this long overdue development was tempered by the sour experience of the police and their gnawing suspicion that something was amiss.

As Lawson's trial date got closer, Bill occasionally asked the other witnesses if they had been spoken to by the police. Their answer was always no.

When the trial took place at the city's district court in September 2010, Bill was startled to learn that he and his son William were the only two prosecution witnesses in attendance. It's not that the Crown Office had chosen to dispense with the other witnesses; instead, they could not use them because there were no statements from them. The police hadn't been near them in the five months since Lawson's arrest.

Lawson's defence lawyer asked Bill whether there were

any other witnesses to the threat apart from him and his son. Observing the legal maxim to never ask a question which you don't know the answer to, the lawyer had read that Bill had named other witnesses in his statement.

When Bill responded that, yes, there were several other witnesses, the lawyer then asked him where they were. Bill could only shrug his shoulders and offer back that he had no idea – it was really up to the police to explain. This exchange served the defence purpose of casting 'reasonable doubt' on the innocence of Lawson.

The court also heard from Bill's son who, he admits, did not perform well in the unfamiliar and oppressive environment, but nonetheless would hardly be seen as entirely independent. The justice of the peace duly concluded that Lawson was not guilty.

Feeling that he had been denied justice, Bill was furious. He believes the case had been lost before it had even begun because of the police's failure to contact the other witnesses. Had they given statements and been cited to testify, he reasoned, then the outcome may have been different.

Bill believes the police deliberately failed to speak to the witnesses for the same reason that they had spent so long doing nothing. Namely, that convicting Lawson of the threat would put a bright spotlight on the utter inadequacy of the fire investigation and would give traction to Bill's complaints.

He genuinely feels that the police were working to this hidden agenda. The threat allegation had been a loose end that Bill was not letting them ignore, so the next best thing was to effectively sabotage the case through inaction while being able to deflect criticism by saying that they had done their job by charging him.

Anyone who has suffered an injustice at the hands of police in Scotland is soon taught a lesson in the difficulty

of achieving meaningful redress. Incredible reserves of
patience and determination are needed for those who
have been wronged. Complaints are routinely met with
a head-spinning combination of bluffed denials, obfuscation and a dishonest selectivity about what is in dispute,
with incriminating weak points being overlooked sometimes in favour of the banal. A commonly used rebuttal
is when Officers A, B or C 'do not recall' events, usually
relating to a colleague in the frame and enough to kill
stone dead a valid complaint. By far the most cynical
and effective weapon deployed by police forces guilty of
negligence or misconduct is time itself. Victims are sent
into a 'hall of mirrors' complaints process where clear
accusations are buried beneath a barrage of long-winded
letters written in the strange hybrid of management and
police speak apparently expected of those who reach the
rank of inspector upwards. Logic and common decency
are left behind and even crystal clear evidence of derelic-
tion or corruption can be stymied by filibustering officers
who know that once they move on, promoted or retired,
they'll leave ageing complaints in their successor's in-tray.

This is not to blame the thousands of ordinary
hard-working police officers who have to deal with society's dregs every time they go on shift. At fault is a culture where accountability is a stranger.

It can take years to negotiate and the police know fine
well that many will lose patience to continue. It takes a
particular type of person to keep fighting, to allow their
lives to be consumed by a police complaint. Perversely,
this tenacity can then be used against them – as evidence
of obsessiveness. This is exactly what happened to Bill.

Eventually, those who complain are herded into the
arms of the Police Investigations and Review Commissioner
(PIRC), a quango hailed as 'independent' when created in
2013 but, in reality, suspected by many as an extension of

Scotland's cosy police family. In 2015, investigative journalist Paul Hutcheon of the *Sunday Herald* revealed that almost 75 per cent of PIRC senior investigators were ex-police.

Bill could fill a filing cabinet with the amount of correspondence he has accrued from numerous senior officers. In relation to the police failures over the Lawson threat allegation, it took Bill more than seven years to finally chisel a confession of wrongdoing from Police Scotland. It was blatant. They should have held their hands up straight away.

The admission came from Detective Chief Inspector Andrew Edward. In a nine-page letter dated July 2016, the senior officer admits that DC Martin should have raised a crime report for the threat allegation and that he should have traced and interviewed the witnesses.

Edward wrote that Bill's interview of 12 November 2009 'should have been regarded as you reporting this [Lawson fire threat] as a crime and should have been recorded as such'.

Edward goes on to say that hapless Martin was not entirely to blame because he had not been specifically instructed to take these actions by two senior officers. By this late stage in the saga, both these officers had retired so could not offer any explanation, providing the police with a convenient full stop.

Bill had a quiet chuckle to himself to be reassured by Edward that 'Martin will be spoken to in relation to a knowledge gap in the procedure for the recording of crimes and provided with the corrective advice in this regard'. Seven years too late.

6

FIRE STARTER STRIKES AGAIN

The fire starter stood still and silent in the dark woods, watching and waiting. Chatter and laughter drifted across the quiet, rain-soaked street as Bill and Jackie arrived home from a night out, skipping round puddles with their jackets pulled over their heads.

Soon after, as the house lights went out, a man slipped from the cloak of thick summer foliage into the street's soft glow. A few swift steps took him to the silver Volvo parked across from the house. Crouching low, he scattered firelighters under the tyres, front and back.

As soon as he turned the little white cubes into yellow blooms he was up and darting across the slick tarmac, back under the trees and into the night.

Bill and Jackie had shared a taxi with a friend, who had dropped them at the end of the street to walk a short distance home. Lager and whisky put Bill to sleep almost immediately, leaving Jackie to potter around the kitchen at the back of the house before flicking out the lights to join him.

It was then that Jackie heard the bang of an exploding tyre. She shot to the front of the house and peered out to see an orange glow reflecting in the wet ground behind her Volvo. Realising instantly what was happening, she ran upstairs, rousing Bill with shouts that her car had been set on fire.

Jackie dialled 999, her heart thundering in her chest, and frantically urged the operator to send firefighters and police.

Wearing her dressing gown, she dashed outside with a bucket of water in a bid to douse the flames, petrified of the consequences if the fuel tank became a fireball. She was joined by Bill and a neighbour with a fire extinguisher. By the time sirens and blue strobes awoke the sleepy cul de sac, the flames were dead, and the charred and smoking Volvo sat lopsided on two melted tyres.

When police arrived, the fire starter was long gone into the woods, which offer numerous escape routes, including toward the path along the Forth and Clyde canal, which runs through north Glasgow, linking Anniesland to Maryhill, Lambhill and Cadder, the home of John Lawson.

Jackie had bought the Volvo S40 new in 2004. It had served her well and, with just 34,000 miles on the clock, had plenty of life left, but it was a write-off. The fire had not spread far but the stench of smoke could never be removed. The intense heat and flames had also caused irreparable damage, rendering pointless any attempted repair.

The attack happened just past midnight on 24 July 2010 – a few weeks before Lawson was tried and cleared of threatening to torch the garage the previous April.

Beneath the blackened wheel were small but obvious remnants of firelighters, which made it thankfully impossible for any police officer to sensibly suggest no suspicious circumstance – as had happened with the garage blaze.

A white-suited forensic specialist worked round the car but the uniformed officers declined Jackie's suggestion

to take a look in and around the woods. They parted with
the familiar promise that the CID would be in touch.

Bill and Jackie had been out with her friends, a close-knit
group mostly comprising SNP politicians, workers and
activists. Jackie had inherited her mother Liz Quinn's
passionate belief in Scottish independence and aspired
to a career in politics. Having begun her working life as
a nurse, she became a businesswoman who spotted an
opportunity in the increased demand for childcare. She
created, grew and sold a children's nursery in the city's
Dennistoun, which did not make her rich but generated
a decent profit.

Jackie was a valued and trusted member of the party
hierarchy in the city. She had been the election agent
for Bill Kidd in 2007 when he first became an MSP and
which saw Alex Salmond replace Jack McConnell as First
Minister, ending Labour's iron grip on Scottish politics.

Jackie came out of semi-retirement to run the busy
constituency office of Kidd's fellow MSP Sandra White,
a long-standing friend of her mother. White had been an
MSP since the Scottish Parliament opened in 1999 and
a list member covering all of Glasgow until she won her
constituency seat in 2011. Sometimes Jackie was entrusted
to stand in when White was busy, taking her surgeries to
hear constituents' woes. Through Jackie, Bill and Sandra
had also become acquaintances, if not friends, and they
would all sometimes socialise as part of a network of SNP
party activists.

That night, Bill and Bill Kidd had sunk pints of Staro-
pramen lager in Coopers, a grand former bank building
that sits on a corner of Glasgow's Great Western Road
bar. It was the group's usual Friday post-work gathering
spot, where talk often, and inevitably, turned to politics.
Bill had learned to smile and bite his tongue, long being

suspicious of any movement with a nationalist agenda, no matter whether the word was prefaced with 'civic'. His negative views were hardened by occasional digs from SNP activists, once drink had lubricated their prejudices, about his British Army career and fighting under the 'butcher's apron', a derogatory reference to the Union flag. It felt no different to the bigotry experienced during the Troubles.

Bill and Jackie had met by chance while she was viewing a tenement flat for sale beside Turnberry Motors and he came over to say hello. At first Jackie was unsure whether the chatty garage proprietor was interested in her or the Mercedes SLK320 which she had bought with some of the proceeds from the sale of her nursery. Having explained that the Mercedes may need some work, Jackie took Bill's number and scrawled hers on an old business card. Two days later, he asked her out for coffee and when they met in a Byres Road café he talked non-stop. She would learn that his incessant talking was not due to first date butterflies . . . as he barely stopped for breath over the following years.

Their relationship began in February 2009 – a few weeks before Bill fell out with John Lawson over the old van. Little did they know that this dispute and its far-reaching fallout would become such a major part of their lives, to the point where it defined them.

Jackie was hard-working, respectable and respecting of the police – never having had cause to question the commonly assumed belief that they were professional and decent, there to give protection. As their lives became gradually consumed by the conjoined criminal vendetta and failures of policing, it is understandable that the relatively new relationship would be placed under immense stress and strain.

When daylight broke over the ruined Volvo, an exhausted

Bill and Jackie waited for the CID to arrive. They were pleased that, as Anniesland was outwith Partick's jurisdiction, it was detectives from Maryhill police station who were coming to see them.

DC Bernadette Walls and DC Steven Crosbie were shown the Volvo and taken into the kitchen, where they were told the full story, starting with the argument over the Ford Transit and Lawson's alleged threat, the garage fire, the razor blade and ending with the destroyed Volvo, via many smaller acts of vandalism in between.

The couple's bitter expressions of betrayal by Partick CID appeared to elicit some sympathy from the two Maryhill officers, who agreed that the longevity and pattern of increasingly serious crimes merited dedicated and focused policing.

As Jackie says: 'They sat in the kitchen and it seemed to me that they could not understand how things had got to this stage. I thought at the time this was a turning point. We felt so relieved that finally someone in the police was listening to us. I was at my wits' end. The attack on my car outside the house really shook me, although I probably didn't fully appreciate how badly the whole ordeal was affecting my well-being.'

Later that day, Bill and Jackie decided to do some detective work of their own by having a look in the small wooded area, the hiding spot of the dangerous individual who had waited for them to come home and go to sleep, and who used fire and knives as weapons.

A few feet in, they spotted an empty box of firelighters and beside it the crumpled cellophane which had contained the flammable blocks. Bill, being forensically astute, carefully dropped the two items inside freezer bags and sealed them from the elements in the hope that, just possibly, they had been left by the fire starter and may therefore yield DNA or fingerprint evidence.

Walls and Crosbie returned to take possession of the makeshift evidence bags but there appeared to be a change in mood, as Crosbie remained mostly mute while the questions asked by Walls made them feel as if *they* were under suspicion.

When they told Walls that they had both found the fire-lighters box, the response was the pointed and repeated suggestion that, perhaps, it had been Bill who had made the discovery alone? An eyebrow was raised in emphasis when Bill and Jackie were asked, more than once, to explain *exactly* where they had found it.

Jackie remembers: 'It was so strange. All of a sudden the tone changed from the day before. We were being asked these odd questions and the implication seemed to be that we were lying and had not found the box. We were perplexed.'

After Walls left, Jackie found the detective's bank card lying beside the front doorstep. Having taken it straight to Maryhill police station, Jackie was surprised not to receive a call of thanks or even an acknowledgement, adding to the feeling that something was not right.

The firelighters were an own-brand box from Morrisons, which was the nearest supermarket to their home. Bill suggested the police could check the store's CCTV to see if the buyer could be identified. He was later told by police that two boxes had been sold on the day of the fire but viewing the footage of both transactions gave an 'inconclusive' result. It felt like a wasted opportunity. If the police had images of the two buyers, why not show them to Bill and Jackie, even if there were long odds of seeing a familiar face?

After her beloved Mercedes had been scratched and her Volvo set alight, Jackie became scared, angry and sickened. She had nothing to do with Bill's business affairs, knew nothing about John Lawson or about any dispute.

During their 15 months together, the spectre of the vendetta was ever present. She'd found love, loyalty and laughter with Bill, but at a high price, as the relationship also brought fear into her life and danger to her door.

The police installed a black box in their home, which when activated emitted a priority 999 response. This intrusive bit of hardware remains in place at the time of writing, almost a decade later. On one occasion, the police requested that it should be returned to them – but they backed down when Bill asked them to put in writing that there was no longer any active risk to their home.

Following the trauma of the late night fire Jackie and Bill initially took comfort from and hope in the sympathetic ears and soothing words of the Maryhill CID officers. But just 24 hours later that hope had disappeared, just as quickly as the ghostlike fire starter. They had no idea what had caused such a sudden and dramatic change, but things were about to become even stranger and more sinister.

7

CAT AND MOUSE

Bill needed a drink. The day after the Volvo fire, he drove a Lexus, a stock vehicle worth around £3,000, to the Lismore pub in Partick to meet friends. He parked the IS200 nearby, to be left and collected at a later date. The shifting of cars from place to place became a necessary tactic, a game of cat and mouse to prevent them being trashed outside the house.

Three days later, Bill and Jackie were in another car driving along Maryhill Road when his phone chirped the arrival of a text. Bill pulled over to read the message, which was from an unfamiliar number and devoid of punctuation and grammar. It said:

> *I'm watching you ha ha you threaten me once now*
> *I'm going to finish you off you fat mouthpiece*

Exactly three minutes later, another text arrived from the same number:

> *You're dead you fucking scumbag*

Another two minutes passed and a third text arrived. It referred to Jackie and suggested the next thing to be set alight would be the home she shared with her elderly dad and schoolboy son:

> *Your birds a cow and her house is getting it next*
> *happy Guy Fawkes how much is your life worth*
> *you fat fuck*

Seven minutes later, another came:

> *That was a nice Lexus*

Before he could point the car towards Partick, where he had left the Lexus, along came a gloating final message:

> *How much has it cost you now ha ha*

When the couple arrived at the Lexus, they saw deep scratches running along the black paintwork and a tyre carved wide open with a blade. The other three tyres were probably spared due to the attacker being disturbed rather than a sense of restraint. Bill knew that, as tempting as it was, replying to the texts would be a mistake, as the sender would want to get inside his head, to make him angry and force a reaction.

Anyone can issue anonymous threats. While the contents of these messages were alarming, they were also revealing. The sender perhaps didn't realise how much he had given away in just 60 words.

Most obvious was an admission of committing the Lexus attack. And not only was the terrifying threat to set fire to Jackie's home a serious crime in itself, it also alluded to the sender's guilt over the Volvo fire.

The description of Bill as a 'mouthpiece' suggested the sender knew he'd been talking to the police. At this time, John Lawson had been charged and was weeks away from standing trial – and being cleared – for making threats to burn down the garage.

In addition, the question about how much Bill's life was worth could be construed as an extortion attempt, to pay up and all this will stop, which was also a serious crime.

One of the messages seemed to confirm Bill's suspicion that he was being stalked. Either that or some kind of tracking technology had been used to pinpoint where the car was parked.

Small devices, with long battery lives, can be stuck to the underside of vehicles and transmit precise positions to a phone. These little boxes have moved out of the criminal underworld onto Gumtree.

Bill received the texts in Maryhill, while the Lexus was in Partick. When he phoned Patrick and said that Maryhill detectives were already dealing with the Volvo fire, they told him to contact them. One might think that texts containing sinister new crimes and clear evidence tying the sender of the messages to previous crimes would cause the police to sit up and pay attention. Unfortunately not. Arriving at Maryhill, Bill and Jackie noticed a very different attitude from DC Walls. Gone was the support and sympathy she'd shown them after the Volvo fire.

Once Bill had explained about the texts and the Lexus, he was invited into the back of a CID car to go and show them the damaged car in Partick, but when Jackie attempted to join him she was met with a terse instruction to stay put; it was just him they needed. Jackie was not perturbed – she was happy to return home.

The stress of being serial crime victims had gradually coloured Jackie and Bill's relationship. For all that, Jackie did not blame Bill for what was happening – and never did, despite all their shared difficulties – it brought an inevitable strain between them. Too often, the topic dominated their conversations and overshadowed not only the good things in life but the everyday normality that most people take for granted. Then there was the damage it inflicted on Jackie's family and professional relationships. Again, this was not Bill's fault, but it was inevitable that such pressure caused occasional flashpoints of resentment and raised voices.

Bill sat in uncomfortable silence, puzzled by the police's attitude, and by the chunky folder of documents on the dashboard, as Walls and a male detective made their way to Partick. The CID pair relieved two uniformed officers standing guard, then Walls turned her attention to Bill.

She began by asking whether anyone had witnessed him parking the car there. Bill replied no, but could not fathom the relevance of the question. Next were unexpected queries about the status of the vehicle's insurance.

She then asked why he had parked it there instead of at home. Given what had just happened to the Volvo, this was equally strange, but he explained everything – again.

The male officer stood throughout the pavement interrogation with his arms folded across his chest, not speaking a word but saying plenty with his eyes, as they measured Bill and darted glances towards Walls, who held the folder across her chest like a barrier.

Bill was running out of patience. He had suffered crime after crime after crime. It had cost him hundreds of thousands of pounds. His business premises were destroyed. His relationship with Jackie was under strain. They feared for the safety of their children. For over a year he had been forced to waste energy fighting with the police. Throughout, the police had maintained a stance of complete indifference.

After their despair at Partick CID, Bill and Jackie had been elated when Maryhill detectives became involved with the Volvo fire. Their elation had taken a knock with the officers' change in attitude when they returned a day later to collect the firelighter packet found in the woods.

Now, standing beside a trashed Lexus and with texts containing death threats and proof of a vendetta in his pocket, Bill could see that his initial hopes had been misplaced.

Things were not getting better, they were getting worse. No longer were the police being merely lazy or disinterested. Instead, Bill felt barely-concealed hostility and suspicion directed towards him.

Bill remembers: 'After the Volvo fire the two Maryhill cops listened to us in the kitchen and you could see that they finally understood what we had been through. When they collected the empty firelighter box the next day it was clear that something had changed, but by the time of us reporting the Lexus damage and the texts, it had got even worse.

'The male officer didn't speak a single word to me, he just eyeballed me; it was almost as if he was trying to intimidate or unnerve me. They were treating me like I was a criminal. I actually asked if there was something amiss, was there anything I should know? At one point I asked "Are you having a laugh?" because I was so confused and angry about it all.'

Bill provided a formal statement and was assured that a thorough investigation would take place, although bitter experience had taught him not to expect a sudden outbreak of detective work.

There are many things that can be done with a phone number that has been used in the commission of a crime. Police can use network masts to pinpoint where a handset is at any particular moment, including the times calls and texts are made. They can also acquire from networks a list of all numbers called or texted. In turn, the same checks can be made of those numbers, opening up potentially infinite new leads.

It can be established how and where a phone's credit has been topped up. The use of a credit or debit card may reveal a user's identity. Even cash top-ups can be useful, as police can attend the shop, speak to staff and check for CCTV of the transaction.

Most obviously, they can establish who owns the number. Smart criminals tend to use unregistered pay-as-you-go numbers for communicating with other criminals, arranging illicit deals, making threats. In this case, police made an unexpected discovery. It took six weeks, but network T-Mobile told them the phone *was* registered and supplied the male owner's name and address in the town of Halifax, Yorkshire.

West Yorkshire police visited the address on behalf of their Glasgow colleagues and found that the registered user was not there and his name was unknown to residents and neighbours. The most logical conclusion was that the number, in the form of a SIM card, had been bought in an online market such as eBay and the registered name was probably bogus.

By the time the police request for information about the number's top-up history yielded a result, three months had elapsed.

The police were told that the phone number had been bought with £5 of credit on it, used only to send the five texts to Bill and had not been topped up since. They got round to delivering this news to Bill a month later. The case was closed. A senior officer took the decision that no further checks were to be made.

During the four months this all took, Lawson had been cleared of making threats to burn the garage the previous April – the case against him having been fatally weakened by the police failure to speak to Bill's independent witnesses.

8

TO THE BRINK

'Do you think Bill's starting the fires himself?'

Jackie was at work in the constituency HQ of SNP politician Sandra White when her mum, Liz Quinn, casually aired the theory. Liz had been asked to work for a few hours on the MSP's payroll, helping out by doing odd jobs in the busy office which Jackie had run for three years.

Jackie was not shocked by the question because it seemed so ridiculous, but she was puzzled as to how it had even entered her mother's head.

In response, Jackie pulled a face and told her not to be so daft, but her accompanying smile was unconvincing.

Jackie's mum called Bill her 'car fairy' in gratitude after he sourced her beloved Honda, its raised driving position helping to alleviate the pain of her arthritis. Just before the Volvo fire, all three had gone for an Italian meal to celebrate Liz's birthday. They had a decent relationship, but Jackie had been noticing a change creeping into her mum's attitude towards Bill. Perhaps maternal protection was a factor. What mum would be unconcerned about a daughter's involvement with someone who was subject of a criminal vendetta? However, where it had previously just been a sense of her mother's antipathy, Jackie was now certain of it. Liz's suggestion – that Bill would destroy his own business and vehicles – was made on the Monday immediately after the Volvo fire.

Sandra White had made similar and equally puzzling comments to Jackie, suggesting that Bill might be more trouble than he was worth. The politician was Jackie's employer but also a family friend reaching back 20 years; Liz Quinn had been a staunch supporter of the SNP during the decades when the party could only dream of power.

Jackie's relationship with her mother was strong, but it would be no exaggeration to say that the strength of her political bonds were as solid and meaningful as those between mother and daughter. When faced with constant questions and comments about Bill from those she most loved and respected, it hurt deeply. Jackie was a capable and independent businesswoman but those qualities are no shield from universal human frailties. It is no contradiction to be strong and capable while also being prone to crippling periods of darkness and self-doubt. For Jackie, there had been episodes during her adult life of anxiety and depression. Her fraught relationships stoked and provoked those feelings.

But White and Bill got on well (although she did regret spurning his advice not to buy a temperamental Alfa Romeo from him. Her determination to purchase the £2,000 car was clinched because its registration plate contained her SW initials and her year of birth.) She asked Jackie for the names of the police officers dealing with the Volvo investigation and vowed to make representation on her behalf, as she would for any constituent who sought help.

White spoke to DC Bernadette Walls by phone and told Jackie they'd discussed what assistance the MSP might be able to offer, even just moral support. Interventions by MSPs often have an immediate effect on senior officers' decisions about the level of effort, time and resources they devote to a particular investigation.

Meanwhile, little did Jackie know that after the Volvo fire, Lexus attacks and text threats she was on the brink of being suspended from work, ostracised by friends and party colleagues, and that she and her mum would speak their last ever words together.

At the end of the dramatic week which started with her Volvo being set on fire, Jackie was asked to meet White in a social setting. Over coffee at the Sir John Moore pub in the city centre, the politician told Jackie that she had again spoken to the police at Maryhill. Given that the criminal had somehow been able to locate the Lexus, and also the reference to Jackie in one of the five texts, there were concerns about her being followed to work. The last thing anyone wanted was for the vendetta to spread to the MSP's office.

White again expressed disquiet about the trouble that had been present throughout Jackie's relationship with Bill.

The following week, White went on holiday with fellow SNP MSP Tricia Marwick, who would later be installed as the Scottish Parliament's presiding officer. While the politicians were away in Portugal, Jackie's mum decided she had more to say about Bill. Liz came up behind Jackie in the office and gently placed her hand on her shoulder, a steadying act to prepare her for important words.

Liz had previously only gone as far as asking whether Bill might be to blame for what was happening. This time there were no gentle questions and suggestions, rather a blunt command for Jackie to split up with Bill. 'I think that Bill is a gangster,' Liz told her eldest daughter. 'He's causing all this trouble and you need to get rid of him.'

Jackie's emotions wavered between anger, incredulity and mirth. Anger won. She snarled at her mother not to be so damn stupid, to mind her own business and keep her ridiculous opinions to herself. Liz shook her head and walked out the door of the Baltic Chambers building in Wellington Street. It was the last conversation they ever had.

Jackie wished she'd probed her mum to try and establish *exactly* where the suggestion was coming from. She feels that, had she done so, the entire course of future events may have changed. She believes that had the truth emerged at this point, her family and friends in the SNP would have supported her and Bill as they waged a painful, lengthy and costly fight for justice. Instead, they turned their backs.

Jackie shook with anger in the empty office. Bill and she had been through the ordeal of a sustained crime vendetta, through no fault of their own, and rather than comfort and support from her mother she was being ordered to end her relationship, as if she were a naughty or naive teenager going out with a boy from the wrong side of the tracks.

The SNP was still smarting from recent newspaper revelations that Nicola Sturgeon, then Deputy First Minister, had urged a judge to spare a wealthy fraudster from prison. Sturgeon's criminal constituent had stolen £140,000 from taxpayers, and already had a similar previous conviction, yet she penned a letter describing his crimes as 'a mistake'. This ill-judged intervention led to calls for Sturgeon to resign and the episode served as an Icarus-style warning to the party's other MSPs about the danger to their careers of flying too close to criminals. Was this near-miss for Sturgeon a factor in White's position?

Jackie and Bill had also been arguing constantly. In their relatively short relationship, they had suffered the garage fire and been sent the razor blade in the post, her car had been destroyed and the other crimes against them had been compounded by chronic police failings.

Their daily lives had been entirely consumed by crime and the wearying battle with the police. The consequent stress of maternal disapproval and strained relations with her SNP kin magnified the burden which eventually grew to a point where reason and control were lost.

Drained and confused, Jackie had reached breaking point. With her career and maternal bonds now virtually broken, she felt isolated and impotent. She travelled to the Menzies Hotel, which sits beneath the Kingston Bridge running high above the River Clyde as it flows through the city centre. Bill had no idea where she was, nor that her mind was crowded with thoughts that there was only one way out, one devastating and final release from her agony. She reasoned that taking her own life in an anonymous hotel room would be better than 'tainting' the family home where her dad and son lived.

Jackie remembers: 'I was at rock bottom and it seemed that suicide was the answer, the only answer. I was totally depressed. Bill and I were having a lot of fights and I just couldn't think straight. I needed to shut myself off from everything – my family, my mum, Bill, work, the police. I was unwell, I was not thinking clearly, but at the time it made sense, it seemed logical, even to the point that if I was going to do it, it should be away from the house, somewhere anonymous and impersonal.'

Bill bombarded Jackie with calls and texts, which became increasingly frantic as she failed to reply. Her disappearance was completely out of character. As the rising sun reflected on the River Clyde, Jackie awoke to find dozens of messages and missed calls. Deep down, she knew that death was not the solution and called Bill to explain where she was and why.

Bill raced to the Clydeside hotel, where he found Jackie, red-eyed and broken, but fixable. At that moment, she vowed that no matter how difficult things were, she would share her feelings with Bill rather than withdraw into herself and be consumed by the darkest of thoughts. It would not be the last time she felt this way, as the endless trauma of the saga occasionally sank her into troughs of depression. Next time, she would heed the warning signs and seek help.

Despite being concerned about interrupting White's holiday, Jackie sent an email explaining that she was unwell and was not able to work. Those two days, locked alone in a hotel room contemplating suicide, were her first period of absence through ill health in three years.

Jackie's fragile state of mind was hardly helped by the unexpected response – the suggestion that her time off was inconvenient to the smooth running of White's office. The MSP had also been attempting to call Jackie, but she had been in no fit state to answer. Unable to reach her employee, she then called Jackie's dad, Jack Mills, who was in his eighties and was suffering from the early stages of dementia. He mistakenly informed White that he thought Jackie was away with Bill. To White's ears, did Jack's information sound like Jackie had abandoned the office to galavant off with her lover, the troublesome gangster?

With Bill's support and encouragement, Jackie found the strength to return to work on Friday, 13 August, where she was welcomed back to her desk with a curt email from White. The content was arch and formal, the tone lacking any warmth or compassion. Jackie read it and re-read it, dumbfounded.

> I have contacted HR in Parliament and taken their advice as follows. I request that you attend a meeting with myself in my office at Baltic Chambers on 20th August 10 a.m. to discuss a recent unauthorised absence. You are of course entitled to bring someone to accompany you, if you so wish. Sandra

The email was the first step in a formal sacking process. Jackie was staggered. She could not understand why White – with whom she had intimately shared three years of her working life and had been friends for even longer – could so suddenly turn against her.

In desperation, she wrote an email to another senior MSP, Kenny MacAskill, who at that time was the Scottish government's justice secretary, best known for his controversial decision the previous year to grant the early release of Lockerbie bomber Abdelbaset al-Megrahi.

Sent from her personal email account, Jackie explained to MacAskill her party connections, although she stressed that 'this matter is personal' and adding, 'I'm contacting you as a last resort.'

As she explained in her email:

> Myself and my partner have been the victims of a deranged stalker since last November. He has burned my partner's garage business down, he has destroyed/ vandalised cars, sent a razor blade in the post to our family home, where we live with my 82-year-old father and 15-year-old son.
>
> The latest events are that he burned my Volvo outside our house on 24 July, the car has now been written off by my insurance company, he has also sent texts to my partner threatening that the house will be next, threatening his life, asking how much his life is worth etc.
>
> We have been pressuring the police to take action against this person since the garage fire last November. The case has been dealt with originally by Partick CID, who basically did nothing, but since my Volvo fire Maryhill CID have now taken over.
>
> The garage fire was not investigated despite us both giving statements on the night of the fire that we strongly suspected arson. There has been a constant

stream of attacks on us for the past 10 months and yet
this man is still walking the streets.

We have spent the past 10 months trying to get
the police to take us seriously and to take some action
against this person. We've been told that the forensics will take months to complete. In the meantime, I
cannot sleep at night for fear of my house being set on
fire during the night. The police asked me if there was
anywhere else we could go in the meantime!

I desperately need help with this situation. I can't
deal with this much longer.

Jackie offered to meet MacAskill in order to better explain,
adding: 'I would just like you to be informed as to what
it's really like to be the victim of crime, which the police
do not treat seriously or with the urgency it deserves.'
She warned that the crime campaign could 'end up as a
murder case, if things are not followed through quickly'
and the prediction that 'either my partner/myself or a
family member will be attacked by this man or there will
be deaths when he sets my house on fire. Maybe the police
will take it seriously then'.

Jackie ended her email to MacAskill with an emotional
plea: 'Can you please help me?'

Apparently not. She did not receive an acknowledgement, let alone a reply. Later, MacAskill's office said they
had not seen the email.

As White's office manager, one of her duties was to write
and dispatch press releases on the politician's behalf,
which led to her becoming a member of the National
Union of Journalists.

Jackie contacted the union to seek their advice about
White's 13 August email instructing her to attend the
meeting on 20 August. Union representative Fiona
Davidson agreed to join Jackie for the 10 a.m. meeting,

but it was over before she had even arrived. Jackie had been ordered out – and relieved of her work phone and office security pass – by 9.05 a.m.

Jackie remembers: 'I arrived at work at 9 a.m. as usual, when Sandra appeared and started ordering me to not sit down, not to go near the computer. She was shouting that I was leaving the office and that I was suspended for taking unauthorised time off. I was already in a very fragile state and I just couldn't believe what was happening. The way Sandra treated me was dishonourable and disgraceful.'

The next day, Jackie received a letter from White. The MSP had initially told her that the reason for the meeting was her alleged unauthorised absence. However, the formal letter introduced a new allegation. Jackie read the correspondence with astonishment. 'You have corresponded on my behalf regarding a constituent [Bill] who I understand is your partner, without my knowledge or consent.'

White's letter, heavy with legalese, ordered Jackie to stay out of the Glasgow office and the entire Scottish Parliament building. Failure to obey would be treated as 'gross misconduct'.

On the same day that Jackie was suspended from work, her dad Jack was taken by his youngest daughter Anne on a trip to France to visit war graves of family members killed in past conflicts.

When they got back to Scotland, Anne decided to take Jack to her Edinburgh home rather than return him to Jackie, as had been agreed. When Jackie opened the front door to welcome home her father, he made his way up the driveway with tears glistening in his eyes. Jack, a quiet and dignified gentleman not prone to outward shows of emotion, wept in his eldest daughter's embrace. As Jack's sobs faded he explained that Anne had put him under pressure with questions about Jackie and Bill's relationship and their domestic and financial arrangements.

Jackie remembers: 'It was horrible seeing him that way. His dementia had just been diagnosed but he was in an absolute mess, confused and emotional. One of the reasons I bought the house in the West End was because I knew Dad would need help as he got older and could live with me. He said Anne had asked all these odd questions about Bill and money. He said that he'd been told to stop paying towards our household bills. This was just after my mum told me to dump Bill because she thought he was a gangster and Sandra suspended me from work. At the time this was all bizarre and inexplicable.'

Appalled at the state of her vulnerable dad, it was the last time that Jackie and Anne spoke. The next day Jack had recovered his composure enough to phone Anne to tell her how upset he had been at her probing and that he intended to defy her by continuing to pay towards the bills.

That call turned nasty. Jack was told, from that moment on, that he should consider he only had two daughters. Jack, who had been a plumber before completing night school classes to become an environmental health officer, passed away six years later in June 2016, having never again spoken with Anne.

9

SISTER ACT

The damage done to the family was not yet complete. Jackie's other sister, Elizabeth Mills, lives in California but was back home for a visit just as the implosion was taking place. Elizabeth was a member of a US duathlon team competing in an event in Edinburgh. Similar to a triathlon but without the swimming, competitors run, cycle then finish with another run. As Elizabeth slogged her way up and around Arthur's Seat, forcing her legs to keep moving and gasping for air while trying to appreciate the grand vista of Edinburgh, she felt a mixture of nostalgia and even misty-eyed patriotism, the kind experienced by expats who have made new lives in other parts of the world.

Elizabeth was the middle of Liz Quinn's three daughters, with Anne the youngest and Jackie the eldest, and during her trips back to Scotland she stayed with her mum. Elizabeth and Jackie were the closest of the sisters and sometimes felt their mother to be overly critical of them and rarely forthcoming with encouragement or praise.

Living more than 5,000 miles away allowed Elizabeth to detach herself from the family dramas in which her mother usually took a leading role. Jackie had told

Elizabeth about the crimes she and Bill had suffered and their problems with the police, but a lid had been kept on their mother's increasingly strident views about her new partner. During Elizabeth's visit, Liz was intent on sharing these opinions, regardless of whether they were wanted.

Liz summoned Elizabeth out onto the balcony of her flat, where they could speak privately, away from the children. Given the choice, Elizabeth would have preferred to bolt back up Arthur's Seat but suspected that her mother would have likely given chase. Deciding that resistance was futile, Elizabeth shuffled out to the balcony, drawing face to face with her waiting mother, who was poised like a conspirator and began to speak in a stage whisper. What Liz said that day in September 2010 is further evidence that she viewed Bill as a criminal.

Elizabeth, speaking about the encounter eight years later, recalls: 'My mother took me outside because she wanted to say something without my kids there. It was odd and awkward because I was there for a holiday. She spoke very quietly and with a gossipy tone of voice. It was almost whispered, as if to give it importance. She believed that Bill was a criminal and bad news, and that I should stay away from him. She suggested that I would be in some kind of danger and wanted to know if I knew anything – which I didn't. I think she believed what she was saying. It may sound strange, but I think she kind of wanted to. Mum liked pointing out anything bad we did and was always critical. In such circumstances, a mother should have wanted to help, but the way she went about it was more critical of Jackie's personality and her integrity.

'She was acting like Bill posed a danger to us. It was kind of crazy. I was curious as to how she was coming up with all this, but I didn't ask any questions because I felt really uncomfortable talking about my sister.

'It was a one-way conversation and lasted about ten minutes. I don't just take someone's word, especially not my mother's, as gospel. At the time I didn't say anything to Jackie because I didn't want to cause any distress. I really just pacified my mum and acted dumb. I don't think Jackie holds anything against me for not telling her. Jackie has always been pretty protective of me and I didn't want to get involved.'

Not long after Elizabeth returned to California, her marriage came to an end. To her disbelief, her mother offered sympathy and support to her estranged husband. The relationship between Elizabeth and her mum was already strained, but this betrayal caused it to snap. Just like Jackie, Elizabeth never spoke to their mum again.

Many years later, once a fuller picture emerged, Elizabeth told Jackie all about the strange episode in which her mother had whispered poison in her ear.

She provided a sworn legal statement which said:

> On my visit to Scotland in September 2010, my mother Liz Quinn informed me that Jackie's boyfriend Bill Johnstone had an extensive criminal record/background. Liz Quinn stated that her friend, MSP Sandra White, had access to this information and that I should not associate with my sister due to this.

Jackie wishes that Elizabeth had spoken to her at the time, but fully understands her reasons for not doing so – namely to avoid being dragged into an episode of their mother's soap opera.

Jackie recalls: 'Elizabeth came home to this family storm to be told that Bill was some kind of gangster. She assumed that I must have been aware of this, so thought it best to say nothing.'

Had the truth come out then, perhaps the family schisms

could have healed before they became broken beyond repair? Elizabeth remains willing to speak to Police Scotland about what she was told – although they have never taken up the offers to do so.

10

THE ARMY: YELLOW CARD

Margaret Thatcher had been in Downing Street a matter of weeks when the British Army suffered its biggest loss of life in the Troubles, as the IRA slaughtered 18 soldiers with two massive roadside bombs. Hours before the massacre at Warrenpoint, the IRA blew up the Queen's cousin Lord Louis Mountbatten while on holiday across the border in the Republic of Ireland. The bomb on his yacht also killed three others, including his 14-year-old grandson.

It was against this bloody backdrop in 1979 that Bill was sent back to Northern Ireland to lead an eight-man section in the rural badlands of County Tyrone. He was aged just 22 and younger than all of the men under his command, though Bill's maturity, experience and authority silenced any talk that he was too young to lead the older men.

The top brass had seen qualities of leadership and intelligence in the young soldier that informed their bold decision to put him in charge of a rifle section with the two stripes of bombardier, the Royal Artillery equivalent of corporal.

In September of that year, Pope John Paul II addressed a crowd of 250,000 in the Republic, telling them, 'On my knees I beg of you to turn away from the paths of violence and to return to the ways of peace.' The pontiff's plea had no effect; the terrorists' fanaticism, determination, bloodlust and hatred eclipsing their supposed Christian faith. A counter message issued by the IRA declared that 'force is by far the only means of removing the evil of the British presence in Ireland'. It was to get much darker in Northern Ireland before dawn broke.

The 16th Regiment – the Glasgow Gunners – were ensconced in a highly fortified base in Cookstown, the county's fourth largest town after Omagh, Dungannon and Strabane. Despite the verdant rolling hills and picture postcard villages of whitewashed cottages under big skies, it was no safer than dodging inner-city snipers on the mean streets of Derry's Bogside and Creggan.

Low-flying army helicopters – barely skirting the hedgerows – took Bill's section to all corners of the largest county in Northern Ireland. Patrolling rural roads, with the ever present risk of bombs, was to play a lottery with your life.

A few weeks after the IRA rejected the Pope's request for peace, four Royal Artillery soldiers were killed by a remote controlled bomb on a road near Dungannon. The four English soldiers – aged 19, 20, 21 and 23 – were attached to the Glasgow Gunners from another Royal Artillery regiment.

During patrols, Land Rovers took turns alternating as lead vehicle. By chance, it had been the English lads' turn to go first over a culvert when the 1,000-pound bomb was detonated.

Later, a Glasgow Gunner who had been in the rear Land Rover returned from a foot patrol to find a bullet hole through the groin of his trousers. Unscathed on both occasions, he earned the nickname 'Lucky'. No one liked standing next to him.

The responsibility on Bill's young shoulders was immense; the war was getting dirtier by the day. Bill's new seniority meant that younger soldiers under his command, nicknamed 'sprogs', were given particularly unpleasant or dangerous jobs. Bill had been the sprog when he was ordered to lift the lid off the bomb beside the Creggan gasworks.

During this tour, no longer the sprog, he and his men were called out to deal with a badly decomposed body. The corpse was in the living room of a house and had been slowly roasted beside an electric fire for several days. Deep in a Republican area, there was no time to wait for forensics or any other formality usually associated with an unexplained death. The door was kicked in and two sprogs were tasked with scooping up the half-cooked human remains and tipping them into a body bag. This they did, between bouts of throwing up.

All soldiers are expected to carry the army's rules of engagement – known as the 'yellow card' because of the colour of the paper on which they are printed – which dictates when weapons can be fired and the circumstance in which deadly force is allowed. While the terrorists operated to no recognisable rules – just ask the families of the young men blown to bits at Warrenpoint or the many other victims of cowardly bombing, booby traps and snipers – there is no doubt that in some instances British soldiers paid little heed to the yellow card and people were killed without legal justification.

Despite the extreme danger of serving in Northern Ireland at that time, some of the young soldiers who served alongside Bill had a cavalier attitude. Two Glasgow Gunners sneaked out of the Cookstown base to visit what they thought was a relatively safe pub. As they played pool, a local growled: 'We know you're army, you won't be leaving here alive.' The memory of Captain Robert Nairac – abducted, tortured and killed while leaving just such a pub – weighed heavily in the collective minds of the British military.

One of the soldiers produced his Browning 9mm pistol and fired a shot through the man's head followed by two more into his chest. They then casually stepped over the corpse and walked out the pub. This fatal shooting resulted in the Scottish soldier being imprisoned but – like many others which Bill had direct knowledge of – it does not even feature in the official, supposedly exhaustive, list of deaths during the Troubles. The dead man may have been a blowhard rather than a terrorist, but to have gambled on it would have been reckless, or at least that seemed to be his justification for the shooting. IRA interrogation techniques were short, brutal and effective. One practice was to chop off body parts from a captured soldier. Morphine injections would prevent him from passing out with the pain. Once the required answers were elicited, death was immediate.

Bill recalled: 'If you were captured there was only one outcome – you would not survive. To put your hands up was to die and die badly. That's why you would do anything to prevent being taken.'

Even decades later, deaths at the hands of British troops are still subject to exhaustive police investigation. In 2016, two ex-Paras, by then aged 65 and 67, were charged with the fatal shooting of an IRA man in Belfast 44 years earlier. In 2019, it was announced that another Para, known as Soldier F, would be prosecuted over his role in Bloody Sunday almost half a century prior, being charged with murder and attempted murder. This prompted revulsion in military circles and delight amongst some Nationalists and Republicans, although many felt that others should also have been charged.

During this second tour, Bill witnessed more RUC bigotry. Many of the police officers were honest and brave, living with the same daily risks as the military and threats that were alien to mainland UK officers. While many of these police had no time for sectarian hatred, others wore it as a badge of pride, loudly and bitterly denouncing 'Fenians' and 'Taigs', which jarred with some of the Glasgow Gunners, many of whom were young Catholics from housing schemes that looked just like those of Belfast and Derry.

Two weeks after seeing four colleagues killed by the roadside booby trap, around 20 members of the Royal Artillery were invited to join an RUC Christmas party at a depot shared by the police and army on the outskirts of Cookstown. Beer, Scotch whisky and Irish whiskey flowed as soldiers and police officers, uniformed and plain-clothes detectives put down their weapons and enjoyed festive respite from the relentless hatred outside. The male camaraderie came to an abrupt halt when one Glasgow Gunner stood on a desk and launched into a booming rendition of 'The Wild Colonial Boy' – a folk song about a mythical Irish teenage rebel who ended up being shot dead in Australia. It was clearly not the type of tune normally heard at an RUC bash.

The singer had barely begun when he was rugby tackled by a burly policeman and sent flying through the air. The room erupted, as the Glasgow Gunners leapt to their silenced singer's defence.

Up to 50 people became involved in the testosterone- and booze-fuelled melée – the soldiers outnumbered by around twice as many police. Fists flew and some RUC men flailed wildly with their batons, cracking soldiers' skulls.

When one police officer went for his pistol, two soldiers just back from foot patrol reached for their rifles. The threat of the fist fight becoming a gun fight was enough to cease the violence. Had common sense not returned, it could have become a bloodbath. As it was, the damage was serious enough, with black, blue and bloodied faces and broken bones. That incident, and others where niggles between the police and army turned ugly, were covered up by each side, who recognised the propaganda boost to Republicans of them fighting amongst themselves. The IRA would have been delighted at the early Christmas gift of soldiers and police officers trying to murder each other.

As Bill neared the end of the six-month tour, he was told his section would not be going home but would instead be staying in Northern Ireland for a further three months, taking him into 1980. Stationed in Girdwood Parks barracks in north Belfast, they joined other regiments and patrolled the staunchly Protestant enclave of Tigers Bay, an interesting experience for Bill, as his father's family had roots in the area. He found red, white and blue sectarian bile just as hard to stomach as the green, white and gold variety.

As a section commander, Bill routinely received and shared intelligence with other branches of the army. Huge effort was put into harvesting and disseminating raw information from the streets of Derry and villages of Tyrone.

He carried with him a book of photos of the most wanted terrorists from both sides of the religious divide. The ever-changing booklet featured possible 'players', such as Martin McGuinness and Gerry Adams, who later became mainstream politicians and eventually members of government following the 1998 Good Friday Agreement.

Section commanders received visits from members of the army's shadowy intelligence units, who were pleased to glean anything about known terrorists, such as photos, cars they drove, the company they kept or any other hard-won snippets that would help to paint a picture of the enemy.

This was not a conventional war. The enemy wore plain-clothes, they hid within communities; they most certainly did not carry yellow cards or observe any conventional rules of warfare. The British government eventually learned that they could never prevail through the blunt imposition of military might, which so far had served only to alienate communities and fuel hostilities.

During this period, the Troubles evolved to become more opaque. Many factions of the army and security services were at play, each one immersed in a necessary culture of secrecy. They worked furtively and independently of each other with little interest in what their comrades were getting up to. Bill refused to trust RUC Special Branch. In turn, the police would keep its own secrets from the army, which in itself had competing rival units and egos.

Only a handful of the very most senior personnel, including the Prime Minister and Home Secretary, would have a complete overview of this otherwise impenetrable landscape. The next time Bill returned to Northern Ireland, he too would be spending time in the shadows.

11

NOT INTERESTED

Bill and Jackie stepped out of the icy November night and through the heavy wooden swing doors of Coopers bar. As they zig-zagged and excused their way through the noisy throng of Friday night drinkers, they spotted the MSP Bill Kidd in his usual spot with a pint in hand, his back towards the door, holding court to a group of SNP acolytes. According to Bill and Jackie, as soon as they drew level with the seated MSP, he threw both hands in the air and barked, 'Not interested!', silencing them before a word had left their mouths. Jackie had been suspended by Sandra White for almost three months by this point and Kidd had become involved in the lengthy disciplinary process.

A central plank of the case had become White's claim to have told Jackie that she was unable to represent Bill because he was her partner. Jackie had pointed out that White's supposed concern about a potential conflict of interest made little sense: Jackie had done work on cases on behalf of White's own daughter and some of her friends. While the slow disciplinary process plodded along, White produced a letter from Kidd backing her position. The suggestion was that White had told Jackie to take Bill's case to Kidd. According to Kidd's letter,

'Mrs White felt that there could be a perceived conflict of interest in her representing the partner [Bill] of her own employee [Jackie].' The letter, on Scottish Parliament headed paper, concludes: 'I was not approached by Ms Mills nor Mr Johnstone regarding taking on his case and therefore cannot add to knowledge of the circumstances of its present standing.'

On occasions where an MSP feels the need to pass a case to a colleague, they would typically inform all parties involved and forward the relevant file. None of this happened. Jackie remains adamant that they never approached Kidd for assistance because it was quite clear that White *was* dealing with Bill's case.

Jackie had been Kidd's election agent – a trusted position which places legal responsibility on the holder to ensure the good conduct of a political candidate's campaign. There is a photo of them together, grinning widely, on the night of his election as an MSP in 2007. Kidd was so impressed by Jackie that he recommended her professionally to Sandra, who duly hired her immediately after the election. Jackie and Bill had often socialised with Kidd and other party members. Indeed, they had been in Coopers four months earlier on the night firelighters were placed under Jackie's Volvo.

Kidd's letter angered, puzzled and upset Jackie. Bill had phoned Kidd's office to try to discuss its contents, but the MSP was in no mood to talk and twice their calls ended abruptly. Bill was therefore not going to pass up the opportunity afforded by this chance encounter, as he and Jackie dotted between various pubs that winter's night in 2010. He was certainly not going to pay heed to Kidd's exclamation of disinterest.

With the cold dispassion learned from life in the army, Bill soberly told Kidd that he would need to discuss the letter, which he described as 'a pile of fucking shite'. One of Kidd's entourage piped up and informed Bill that they were *trying* to have a drink in peace.

Displaying the tact and diplomacy learned from his years in the military, Bill responded by fixing him with a hard stare and telling him, 'Shut the fuck up.' A second member of the group appeared intent on speaking, but Bill pre-empted this with another barrack-room order. 'You can shut the fuck up as well,' commanded Bill. He concluded with an explanation that he would speak to Kidd about the letter another time, then walked out with Jackie to find another pub – without any MSPs in it.

It had hardly been a masterclass in diplomacy by Bill, but the shaken politician and his friends decided that their encounter required the police to be called. Two uniformed officers turned up at Coopers and listened to what each of the group had to say, writing it down in their notebooks. Having done so, the police decided that no crime had taken place and, therefore, no action needed to be taken.

They did not think it even necessary to speak to Bill, who would have been bemused had he even known they had been called. Bill was in for a surprise. For someone in the police was to decide that this petty spat with Kidd was worthy of further attention – a full two months later.

When a pair of police officers arrived at Jackie and Bill's home in January 2011, he thought they were there to provide an update about one of the many crimes the couple had suffered. Instead the police charged Bill with breach of the peace and with making a threat to 'slash' Kidd in Coopers. Upon hearing the charges, Bill was rendered uncharacteristically speechless.

He is not the type of man who lets his mouth run off in pubs and doesn't tend to make threats. He is quietly capable of inflicting effective violence without bravado. The police were making out as if he were a thug who didn't know right from wrong.

In the immediate years after leaving the army, he may have overreacted in such circumstances. Bill himself describes the process of leaving behind his ruthless army mindset and adapting to the niceties of mainstream society as 'getting normal' and admits that it took him a long time to achieve.

The criminal charge was an incredible turn of events. The police had attended the pub on the night and decided it was just a verbal altercation meriting no further attention. Yet, out of the blue and many weeks later, they had taken it upon themselves to go back to Kidd and seek a full statement. Kidd later expressed surprise at the unexpected overture from the police but dutifully obliged them.

The charges against Bill were groundless, trumped up and farcical. Bill has no doubt that the police's decision to charge him has only one explanation – pure and utter malice. Following the garage fire and initial acts of vandalism, the police response had been characterised by laziness, ineptitude and disinterest. As more crimes were committed, the initial disregard evolved – inexplicably – to become hostile and suspicious.

Two weeks after being charged, he had another unusual brush with the law. Two female officers came to his door and told him he was under arrest. They handcuffed his hands behind his back and led him out to a marked car, in full view of neighbours. It was a Friday afternoon and he was told that he would spend the weekend locked up before a court appearance on Monday morning. The reason? A Mr John Lawson had complained that Bill had made a phone threat against him. The evidence? None. On the journey to Maryhill police station, one of the officers made reference to Bill's threat against a politician. Bemused and confused, Bill was processed at the bar – fingerprinted, photographed and DNA taken – then led to a cell where he was told to make himself comfortable for the weekend. A couple of hours later, the two officers, their manner now civil, returned. They unlocked the door and told him that he was free to go; there had had been a mistake. Perhaps he would like a cup of tea? They even gave him a lift home, during which one of the officers mumbled something about Lawson knowing how to play the system. To be treated this way, on the word of a man who was accused of committing multiple crimes against Bill with impunity, was unacceptable. Yes, the spectre of the Kidd charge explained the police's attitude towards him. But Bill could not help feeling that there must be something else to it – a piece of the puzzle was missing. Immediately on Monday morning, his lawyer Chris Rogers wrote yet another complaint to the police

The only thing Bill was 'guilty' of was being a serial victim of crime. Next to nothing was being done about those crimes. Yet the police were now going after him. He believes that invisible enemies within the police latched on to the Kidd case, which they saw as an opportunity to nail him. That a groundless allegation by Lawson could lead to his arrest was an outrage. But to the police, Bill was a relentless and noisy nuisance who had caused them chaos and grief with a flood of complaints and lawyer's letters, starting after the botched and lazy response to the garage fire.

The police would attempt to use the minor incident in Coopers to try and criminalise Bill and trash his reputation. But although he could not have known it, something good was to come of the police's astonishing conduct.

12

EUREKA I

Weeks later, Bill found himself handcuffed to a police motorcycle on Hyndland Road in Glasgow's West End. Patiently, and repeatedly, he explained to the officers that they had the wrong man – there surely could *not* be a warrant for his arrest. But although he persisted, he was going nowhere, even if he wanted to.

He had been stopped while driving for a routine check of his car's trade plates. These are used in the motor industry to temporarily register vehicles being bought and sold – providing the holder exemption from having to tax them individually. Bill had seen the blue lights appear behind him and had pulled over and got out the car. He was driving with his eldest son and daughter and supplied his name and date of birth when asked, which one of the officers repeated into his radio. Moments later, the officer received a response in his earpiece. He nodded and turned back towards Bill.

'Mr Johnstone,' he said, seriously, 'there is a warrant for your arrest.'

'Are you having a laugh?' Bill replied incredulously.

'No, sir, I am not.'

A steel cuff was then closed around Bill's right wrist and he was tethered to the rear of the BMW motorbike.

'You're fucking joking, pal!' As an innocent man, Bill could have been forgiven for deploying more robust language.

The officer explained that Bill was to be arrested, spend the night in a police cell and appear in the dock of a court the next day.

'I'm going nowhere,' Bill told them. 'Your information is incorrect, so you'd better check again.'

More information arrived via the radio. The warrant had been issued after Bill had allegedly failed to appear at Stirling Sheriff Court on a charge of drink-driving.

'You're wrong,' Bill told them again. 'I've never been charged with drink-driving. I've not been in Stirling for years and I haven't failed to appear at court. Check again.'

Police officers are well used to bluffers and blaggers who put hands on hearts, swore on their children's lives and, with wide-eyed conviction, declared the computer *must* be wrong. They'd heard it all before. But Bill's clear, unequivocal proclamation of innocence was convincing enough to penetrate the white helmets and make the officers pause for thought and tread carefully.

Bill's children, both adults, sat watching in puzzlement, but were told to stay put, that they should not leave. Despite not being physically restrained, the order felt like wrongful detention. Bill stood on public display for almost two hours during which time all he could do was keep a cool head and parrot that what was being alleged was completely false. To the voyeuristic eyes of hundreds of passing motorists, the man handcuffed to a police motorbike was no doubt guilty of *something*.

The police control room disclosed that the drink-drive fugitive wanted in Stirling had a tattoo on his left arm. Bill's raised shirt sleeves showed a tattooed *right* arm, but no ink on the left. The officers arched their eyebrows and suggested this in itself proved nothing.

The officers asked for Bill's previous addresses. To his astonishment, the police confirmed that his past addresses matched up with the wanted man.

The officers clearly did not know what to believe. It would be bad letting him go free if the warrant *was* genuine, but worse to arrest an innocent man. No doubt the potential paperwork generated by such a scenario was a consideration.

Eventually, they took the decision to unlock the handcuffs and concede that Bill *may* possibly be telling the truth. There was just enough doubt in their minds to set him free. They suggested if he wanted to take the matter further then he should attend a police station. They then straddled their bikes and roared off – with no apology proffered.

Bill drove straight to Partick police station, where he had become well known since the night Turnberry Motors burned to the ground 18 months earlier. A uniformed officer at the public counter heard how Bill had almost been arrested due to the false accusation he was a wanted man. He explained what had happened at the roadside and asked what could be done to get to the bottom of it and to put it right.

After 20 minutes in a back office, the policeman returned with a CID officer holding a photo of the real wanted man, who bore no resemblance to Bill.

'You're right! It's not you,' exclaimed the excitable young officer.

Bill could be forgiven for not sharing his surprise. Instead he rolled his eyes.

'I know it's not me, I didn't come here to ask if it might be me – I want to know how it happened and what can be done about it.'

The only solution offered was that he could go away and incur the cost of speaking to a lawyer for advice.

Bill himself initially came up with three possible explanations. The first was that his name and date of birth were similar or identical to the mystery drink-drive suspect. The second was that there had been a computer glitch or communication mix-up between the Stirling court and police which resulted in the warrant somehow being wrongly attributed to him. The third was that someone had stolen his identity and used it while committing crimes. Prior to the garage fire there had been a break-in, in which his driving licence and other personal documents had been taken. With every aspect of people's lives increasingly being stored and shared digitally, all of these early theories had potentially far-reaching consequences. He eventually discovered that none of them were correct.

The day after his near arrest, Bill phoned police HQ, where his call was directed to the force disclosure unit, which deals with the storage and accessing of personal information. He explained what had happened and a week later received a letter from them which offered no explanation or apology, merely the glib assurance that 'the concerns you raised will not reoccur in the future'. The response from the police was far from satisfactory, as Bill had no idea why he had been handcuffed and almost arrested by officers who wrongly accused him of being a wanted criminal. It was hardly the same as a mix-up with your library card. The letter was the equivalent of a shoulder shrug.

Another curious exchange had occurred during Bill's two-hour roadside interrogation. At one point, one officer was speaking into his radio to the control room while trying to ascertain whether Bill was telling the truth. The officer said, 'It's the Johnstone name on the warrant.'

It was a puzzling thing to say, which made no sense at the time. Only later did this piece of the jigsaw fall into place and the startling significance of the comment hit home.

13

EUREKA II

Bill could only stare in open-mouthed and wide-eyed disbelief at the words he was reading. His head spun but he didn't know if he should explode with rage or dance for joy. The document in his grip had arrived days after the bewildering roadside ordeal during which he had been falsely accused of being a fugitive by motorcycle police officers.

Court-appointed sheriff officers had mechanically handed over a sheaf of papers to Jackie at the front door in Anniesland. Jackie shrieked for Bill to come downstairs into the kitchen, where she thrust the documents from her shaking hands. At the top was Bill's citation to appear in court on an assigned date to face trumped-up charges of threatening the SNP MSP Bill Kidd at Coopers bar. Within the pile of ordinary paperwork were two extraordinary sheets. In block capitals, each was headed:

NOTICE OF PREVIOUS CONVICTIONS
APPLYING TO **WILLIAM JOHNSTONE**

Below that was stated:

In the event of you being convicted of the charge(s) in the

complaint it is intended to place before the court the fol-
lowing previous conviction(s) applying to you.

At the kitchen table, Jackie and Bill read silently agog at
the staggering list of Bill's criminal convictions. The litany
of offences spanned almost 20 years, with appearances at
courts in Stirling, Dumbarton and Alloa.

Bill's prolific criminal career began with violence,
specifically assault and assaulting police officers, which is
categorised as a distinct offence. Other convictions were
for forgery – and passing forged documents – although
whether this was counterfeit currency or something else
it did not say.

This was followed by more assaults, and attempting to
pervert the course of justice, although some specifics were
lacking. Also on Bill's rap sheet were numerous motoring
offences – drink-driving, careless driving, driving while
banned and with no insurance.

There was more assault and police assault, along
with breaching bail conditions and terms of probation.
Showing impressive variety, Bill also had a conviction for
theft along with several breaches of the peace.

Bill's life of crime had earned eight separate jail sentences. The only problem was that every single word
was a fabrication. Bill had no criminal record whatsoever. And to top it off, while virtually all of these crimes
had been taking place, Bill had the most iron-clad
alibi possible: he had been serving his country in the
army.

The paperwork showed that the record actually
belonged to another man called William Johnstone, with
a different date of birth and middle names to Bill.

Initially they assumed that the attachment of the criminal record to Bill's citation had been a simple mix-up.
Perhaps some office worker had thought it applied to him

because the names were similar? But as they read further
they saw that this was no administrative mistake. The documents showed that the criminal William Johnstone used
multiple aliases, including Duncan Johnstone, Donald
Cameron, William Brown, William Stone and Peter
Townsley. The seventh – most recent – alias added to the
record was Bill's full name and date of birth.

This meant that whenever Bill provided his details, as
he had to the motorcycle officers, the police computer
connected his real ID with one of the aliases used by his
criminal namesake.

So not only was this William Johnstone a crook with
an ugly history of violence and dishonesty, he had given
the police a bogus date of birth, which is a crime in itself.
This explained the motorcycle officer's comment 'It's
the Johnstone name on the warrant' while speaking to
the control room operator, who could see the long list of
aliases and convictions.

William Johnstone, the hard-working, honest, deco-
rated former army officer no longer existed. In his place
stood William Johnstone, serial criminal.

This dangerous lie was considered the truth in the eyes
of the state – of every single police officer, Crown Office
prosecutor, member of the judiciary and court clerk. In
today's era of digitised personal data, it raises worrying
questions about the accuracy of the vast amounts of information held about everyone.

As Bill explained: 'The arrival of these documents told
me that my real identity had effectively been stolen by
the police and then applied as an alias to a criminal. I
had been turned into a ghost; my true identity no longer
officially existed.'

In addition, despite the convictions not being recent,
the existence of a live arrest warrant suggested the criminal remained active. Bill's eureka jolt was tempered by

ambivalence. While understandably furious at being smeared, he was also relieved that finally – in his hands – was proof that something was far from right.

He had long suspected that the police's indifference, inaction, coldness, hostility and suspicion over almost two years made no sense. Well, now it did.

As Bill recalled: 'My initial reaction to Jackie was "For God's sake, this is what it's all really about!" I was hopping up and down saying "Yes!" because I had it – I could finally see what had been going on. Any cop looking me up would see a liar, a violent scumbag, a lowlife and a dog. The convictions for police assault were particularly toxic. They would no doubt treat me accordingly.'

There was also a pleasing irony that Bill's discovery only happened because of the police's determination to go after him by resurrecting the Kidd complaint. That decision to charge Bill, and the subsequent Crown prosecution, directly led to his receipt of the bombshell documents, as it is standard practice to disclose criminal records to the accused prior to trial.

Had the police not taken the decision to dust down the Kidd case and use it as a weapon, Bill would have remained blind to the odious record that clung to his good name like a tumour.

But this was far from the end of it. The battle with the authorities had only just begun and Bill's mind buzzed with questions. Was the police's decision to resurrect the Kidd case driven by their belief that he had an extensive criminal record? After all, the Crown prosecutor who decided whether to try him would have taken these previous convictions into consideration with a prosecution less likely if the accused was 'clean'.

Exactly how many times had police officers looked at the record when Bill reported the many crimes? He is convinced that their attitude towards him was poisoned by the record and needed to know exactly who had accessed it and when.

Had the police shared the inaccurate information with anyone else? Bill and Jackie believe that it or its general tone was leaked, which directly resulted in her family fall-out and her being sacked and ostracised by the SNP.

What other information was being held on police computer systems about the man who Bill had now become? It is not just convictions that are stored. The police's Scottish Intelligence Database contains a vast amount of information about suspects – some of it from informants motivated by cash or the cunning to smear an enemy by selling lies to the police. The intelligence attached to Bill could have amounted to anything. He would never know.

Above all else, when and how exactly did Bill become assigned the criminal record?

While Bill accepted that Police Scotland were unlikely to ever voluntarily provide full and honest answers to these and his many other questions, he did not intend to give up.

14

HOLYROOD JUSTICE

SNP politician Sandra White finally sacked Jackie as her office manager following a three-month disciplinary process riven by acrimony and rancour. Minutes taken by Jackie's union representative Fiona Davidson at a hearing three weeks before her dismissal in November 2010 recorded the bitterness. It began with Davidson asking White if it was appropriate for her to decide Jackie's fate, as she was 'effectively the complainer, the witness, the investigator, the prosecutor and now the judge'. White rejected any suggested impartiality but halted proceedings to seek advice from parliament's HR people. Minutes show that when the meeting resumed, Davidson again asked whether White could give a fair hearing, promoting the MSP to snap 'You heard what I said!' The tone descended further when Davidson interrupted Jackie to accuse the MSP of 'smirking'. White responded that it wasn't a smirk but a friendly smile.

Tricia Marwick, White's MSP colleague and holiday companion, was present to assist her and take notes. At this point Marwick accused Davidson of being disruptive, which was countered by Davidson asking exactly what her role was supposed to be.

Jackie pointed out that far from White having nothing

to do with Bill's case, she had taken it upon herself to call DC Bernadette Walls at Maryhill police station to ask about it. The minute records that White 'thought that was irrelevant'. Jackie pointed out that she had also carried out constituency work on behalf of White – for White's own daughter. This seemed to make a nonsense of White's claim that acting for Bill created a conflict of interest. Again, this was dismissed as irrelevant by the politician.

The reason given for Jackie's sacking in November 2010 was that she had allegedly undertaken work for Bill without White's knowledge or consent. The disciplinary process felt like a protracted charade with a foregone outcome, but Jackie could not bring herself to walk away with her reputation trashed. She decided to lodge an unfair dismissal claim to be heard by an employment tribunal. A report in the *Herald* newspaper trailed the case with background information about other employee disputes involving White. It stated:

> In 2006, her [White's] assistant Mark Hirst resigned after issuing a press release in Ms White's name which called the union flag the 'butcher's apron'. Ms White initially disowned the comments, but Mr Hirst later produced an email showing she had effectively signed off the remarks.
>
> A few months later, Ms White put her son Christopher on the public payroll. The *Herald* understands Ms White also had a dispute with another former employee which resulted in a financial settlement for the man concerned.

Jackie was made a similar last-minute offer to settle her case, which would have prevented the tribunal going ahead – but rejected it, as she remained confident of clearing her name publicly.

Her resolve remained intact even though her union decided it would not pay for a lawyer, which forced her to represent herself against White's taxpayer-funded, specialist employment expert from a blue-chip law firm. Pitted against the slick professional, it was an uneven contest, and far from meeting the term 'equality of arms' used by lawyers.

The tribunal took place just weeks after Bill was hit by the thunderbolt revelation that in the eyes of the law he was a dangerous and dishonest serial criminal. His shine as Jackie's star witness was further tarnished with the knowledge that he had just been charged with threatening White's MSP colleague Bill Kidd, no matter how ludicrous the charges would later prove to be. The Coopers contretemps had been caused by the disputed letter provided by Kidd to help back White's employment dispute – but she did not call her Holyrood colleague as a witness.

When Jackie decided that she would cite Kidd, she was informed that the MSP would much prefer to be in a separate waiting room to Bill, which subtly served to further taint his reputation and testimony.

The tribunal took place over a week in June 2011 and at the heart of the dispute was the emailed letter about the Turnberry Motors fire, which had been sent by Jackie to Chief Superintendent Anne McGuire. White told the tribunal she knew nothing of the McGuire email, stating, 'I told her I was aware of the fire because she had told me but I was never aware of any letters being sent from me to the police about it.'

It seems odd that Jackie would email McGuire without White's knowledge or consent – *knowing* that White was to meet McGuire just a few days later. Jackie had even arranged the meeting between them. The admission by White that she had discussed the garage fire with McGuire at the meeting makes her denied knowledge of the email even more odd.

Jackie fought with the parliamentary authorities for a copy of an archived email which she said would prove White authorised the McGuire letter. If the email did exist, it was never shared with Jackie, who told the tribunal: 'It was a chance for me to prove Sandra had sent me an email confirming that I could send the email to Anne McGuire. I know the email was sent.'

The tribunal heard details of the crime vendetta being waged against Bill and Jackie, who put it to her former boss, 'Had she had enough of me with all my problems?' This was denied by White, who professed concern.

It took several months for tribunal judge Walter Muir to reject Jackie's unfair dismissal claim.

He wrote:

> The claimant [Jackie] had indeed been caught red handed being involved in activities which were in defiance of the respondent's [White] clear wishes as well as, potentially at least, amounting to a conflict of interest. The tribunal could readily see that the essential bond of trust had been destroyed by the claimant to the point where it could not be retrieved. In all these circumstances the tribunal regarded the decision to dismiss the claimant as being a fair one.

It was a harsh judicial opinion which shattered Jackie's faith in the system. Anyone entering the lions' den of a court or tribunal quickly realises that loudly shouting 'it's not fair' is not enough to win, no matter how honest and sincere their case.

Employment tribunals are playgrounds where specialist lawyers debate the finest of points and argue the nuances of complex employment legislation, as it is perpetually shaped by case law. A wronged employee can have their claim destroyed on a narrow technicality visible only to an employment lawyer.

Jackie recalled: 'I would have needed to pay to obtain transcripts of the tribunal to even think about an appeal but I had so little money that I was struggling to pay the bills. I had been unemployed for over six months and I had no option but give up. I had made money from the sale of the nursery but that windfall was not life changing and did not last long. Part of the reason for selling was to allow me to buy a larger home, which allowed me to look after my dad full time, rather than put him into care. But I still needed work and before long I was getting pretty desperate. The whole process felt unfair. It was so hard, even though I prepared as best I could. I didn't even know what type of questions I was allowed to ask the witnesses or what was relevant.

'Not only was I up against a leading employment lawyer who knew the system inside out but Bill was my main witness and hc had been falsely smeared as a serious criminal. I now realise that I had no chance.'

Throughout this time, Jackie's mum Liz remained a loyal employee of White and they remained good friends.

As well as being financially stricken through unemployment, taking shifts on a Morrisons supermarket checkout to pay the bills, Jackie watched her dad's health deteriorate. Jack, already suffering from dementia, underwent surgery for prostate cancer. Bill was also feeling the strain, with the onset of a stomach ulcer. Her beloved dad's slow, steady and inexorable demise was another contributory factor in her struggle to maintain good mental health.

On the plus side, Bill and Jackie's stalker had gone quiet, with almost a year having passed since the text threats and Lexus attack. They will never know for sure, but unfortunately the publicity caused by the employment dispute seems to have awoken their tormentor from his hibernation, as he struck again on the very same day that a newspaper published tribunal evidence relating to Bill and the garage fire.

When Jackie and Bill left the house that morning to make their way to the tribunal, they were met with the sight of two destroyed cars, both trade stock. One was a classic Mercedes 190, worth £6,000, and the other was a £10,000 7 Series BMW. A new weapon had been added to their stalker's arsenal in the form of extremely potent chemicals that ate through the paint to reveal bare metal-work. So powerful was the noxious substance that it had burned the glass and melted the plastic of bumpers and trim. Bill had no option but to send the Merc and BMW on a final journey to the scrapyard. To have claimed the losses on his trade insurance policy would have only forced up the premiums to make them unaffordable.

The uniformed police officers who attended seemed dumbfounded at the extent of the damage. They expressed the opinion that it was clearly a serious and targeted attack, not a random act of minor vandalism of the type they more typically dealt with. They were even more convinced when they heard about the long catalogue of previous crimes. Not for the first time, Jackie and Bill were assured that a full investigation would take place. Bill was told by the CID that fingerprint analysis of the vehicles would be done immediately, and took sample prints from Bill and Jackie for elimination purposes. Many years later, Bill discovered that this had not happened; the crime report was closed two months after it was raised. No fingerprints from the cars were ever analysed. It was another missed opportunity.

15

NO CASE TO ANSWER

When police and prosecutors dispense with fairness and due process to deploy the clunking weight of the justice system as a kind of weapon, it is alarming. For them to do so against an innocent man, in a bid to destroy and discredit, ought to be criminal. There should most certainly be consequences.

Bill stood in the dock accused of threatening SNP MSP Bill Kidd in Coopers pub. The judge heard from the politician and the Crown's two other witnesses before bringing proceedings to a juddering halt. Turning to Bill, she told him there was 'no case to answer' and that he was free to go, wholly innocent of what was alleged by the authorities. Unusually, the judge then expressed disquiet about what the case was even doing in court in the first place. The trial was abandoned before a single word was heard from the defence.

The result was unambiguous, although Bill accepts that in the often fickle lottery of Scotland's criminal justice system it could have ended quite differently. Bill was told he was lucky not to have been allocated the adjacent courtroom, where the judge, an apparent SNP supporter, may have been more receptive to the plaintive testimony of Kidd and his two senior party colleagues.

Not only had the police chosen to revisit Kidd's complaint two months after deciding that it did not constitute criminality, but when they submitted their report about the incident to the Crown, attached to it was the extensive – and bogus – criminal record.

The record would have been a significant factor in informing the Crown's decision whether to drop the case or proceed. On paper, Bill was not a middle-aged former army officer with no criminal record but a savage and dishonest serial jailbird with a penchant for inflicting violence on police officers. Now he was threatening a nice politician. What prosecutor would put a red pen through that?

But the Crown had no such excuse to pursue Bill on the basis they thought he was a criminal because he had discovered the existence of the fake record four months before the trial. When Bill's citation revealed this false smear, and he blew the whistle, it should have halted the Crown in its tracks and forced a reconsideration.

Had they done so, it is most likely this thin gruel would have been binned and Bill would have been spared the pressure and uncertainty of being charged, then kept in bail limbo for many long months.

There was another murky aspect to the case which is more abstract and difficult to prove.

Bill was also told by his seasoned legal advisers that the trial may have been sent to the lowly district court because the Crown reasoned there was a better chance of securing a conviction there, the rationale being the perception that JPs who preside in lower courts may be more predisposed to a Crown case than a cynical and streetwise sheriff would be. While most sheriffs would recognise the whiff of a police and prosecution fix, (the theory goes) a non-lawyer JP may not.

Bill's enemies in the police would have been delighted to see him fitted up like the lowlife they – and their computers – said he was. To charge him was to entangle him in the criminal justice process. To convict him of threatening a democratically elected politician in a public place would shut him up and stem his flow of complaints about police incompetence, inaction and corruption.

In the event of conviction, Bill had been warned he could expect to be referred to a higher court for sentencing, where a harsher punishment would be imposed. A jail sentence was perfectly possible.

Another benefit to the Crown of sending the case to a lower court was that they are rarely reported on by newspapers, which means the entire murky episode would take place away from the public gaze, ideal for getting a troublemaker jailed under the radar.

Bill faced two separate charges. The first, and most serious, was that he had threatened violence against the MSP. The second was breach of the peace, a vague charge which the police can throw like confetti, thanks to the elastic definition of any alleged victim feeling 'fear and alarm'.

The threat charge was dropped by the Crown immediately after Kidd, the first witness, gave his evidence. The JP found no case to answer in respect of the more minor breach charge after Kidd's two party colleagues had taken to the stand. One told the court that he did not recognise his police statement.

Jackie had been braced to give evidence in Bill's defence, to explain that she was there that winter's night in the pub and that the incident between former friends amounted to nothing, most certainly not a criminal act. Again Bill and Jackie noted the irony. They had only learned of the fake record thanks to the trial – a trial which would almost certainly not have happened were it not for the record.

*

Bill first contacted me in 2013. He did so because he had read newspaper stories that I had written about police corruption and thought that, as a journalist, I might be interested in investigating and publicising his plight. I left our first meeting with my head spinning by the scale of what had been going on and somewhat sceptical about how much of it was accurate. Over the passing years, I found out that not only was Bill's account truthful but he had only shared part of it during our first tentative exchange, lest the entire tapestry of events bamboozle me.

One of the first things I did was to make a journalistic enquiry to Kidd in which I asked him about the collapsed trial two years prior. This elicited an unexpected response. Kidd confirmed that he had been informed of Bill's acquittal but had no idea that it had resulted in there being no case to answer rather than a verdict of not guilty or not proven.

'Is that what it resulted in,' he replied, 'because no one bothered to come and tell me that, actually? I considered it a threat, maybe he never meant it as one . . . I didn't know if he'd been told to behave himself or whatever.'

The comment – that innocent people may receive some form of ticking off despite being exonerated – may suggest a fairly poor grasp of the justice system by an elected lawmaker.

Even to someone with the backbone, fortitude and life experience of Bill, it is a daunting experience to be ordered to appear before a judge where the case is legitimate, but especially so on trumped-up charges. For Jackie, it was painful and nerve-wracking being on one side of an adversarial criminal trial, set against long-standing friends. She had known Kidd and others in the SNP group for decades, not years. She had been at Kidd's side, nurtured and supported him, in his impressive trajectory from dental hospital receptionist and administrator for White to become an MSP at Holyrood.

Bill was racked with guilt at Jackie's pain. He was also bitterly angry that this non-event, a few angry words in a pub, could result in such a ludicrous, albeit deadly serious, pantomime. By the same measure, half of all Glaswegians would be standing in the dock every Monday morning.

'The way Jackie was being treated by her supposed friends was disgusting,' he recalled. 'Her world had been destroyed and I was absolutely raging. She knew that the case against me was utter nonsense but she was very worried. Had the Coopers encounter happened 15 years earlier I would have probably taken the head off his shoulders, but I've mellowed a lot in recent years. Sometimes I think that's not for the best.'

Above all else was the feeling of complete bafflement. Bill and Jackie knew about the record but still had no meaningful grasp of the scale of what was happening to them. They had no way of knowing how little was being done by the police in relation to the criminal vendetta being waged against them. They could not appreciate that the institutionalised police view of Bill was so warped by the false belief he was a gangster. Bill was on a knife edge. He had got lucky this time, but he realised that he could not put a foot wrong. The police only had to get lucky once.

16

THE ARMY: CAPTAIN NAIRAC

The history books state that Captain Robert Nairac went to his death without giving up any secrets to his IRA torturers and killers. The story, told by the Republicans and accepted by the British, suited both sides. As far as Bill is concerned, it is untrue.

His experience of specialist interrogation training tells him that anyone who suffers extreme acts of torture has a breaking point. Bill is sure that Nairac, who he first met in 1976 on a rooftop OP in Derry, was no different. Nairac was a brave soldier but he also had a reputation as a risk-taking maverick. On the night of his death, he was undercover in a south Armagh pub on a solo mission to acquire information about the IRA. When he left at closing time, a gang of men pounced and he was forced into a car, never to be seen again. Almost half a century later, his remains have never been recovered.

Nairac was awarded a posthumous George Cross the following year, with the citation stating that he suffered a 'succession of very exceptionally savage assaults in an attempt to extract information' but 'these efforts to break his will failed entirely'. While the military was happy to go along with the story of heroics for public consumption, according to Bill they could not be certain and worked on the basis that everything Nairac knew was known by the IRA.

The reason the IRA wanted people to believe that Nairac had stayed silent in 1977 is logical. If the Brits could be duped into accepting his secrets were safe, it may have persuaded them to keep deep cover army personnel and treasured Republican informants in place. If the IRA had gleaned confidential information from Nairac, it suited them to bluff the Brits into thinking the opposite. That way, they could use it to their best advantage at a time of their choosing.

Bill explained: 'Nairac would have been fully aware that he was going to be killed, so does he tell them anything? Hard-wired into every human being is survival. No matter how bad a situation is, people keep hope. In the movies, they will say "Just shoot me" but that is fiction. They will bluff, duck and dive, lie, say anything to buy time. They will also tell the truth. We believed the IRA was lying about Nairac. It had to be assumed that they knew whatever he knew.'

The Derry rooftop introduction to Nairac was the beginning of Bill's journey into the dark game of army intelligence in 1970s and 1980s Northern Ireland, where the stakes were life and death. Much has been written about this secretive dimension of the Troubles. By its nature, getting to the truth is no easy task, as books and newspaper reports often contain a jumble of contradictions, unsubstantiated snippets and bigotry-fuelled propaganda.

In the early 1970s, the army ran a laundry business in Belfast as a front for intelligence gathering in Republican communities. When the IRA learned the laundry's true purpose, fatal attacks on it followed and it was immediately shut down. The army learned to get smarter, more cunning.

By the late 1970s, another top secret unit was becoming increasingly active. Depending who you speak to, it was called the Force Reconnaissance Unit or, more benignly still, the Force Research Unit. Not that you would find either name on a brass plaque, letterhead or soldier's ID. Those drafted into the FRU would often maintain their status with their original regiment. The FRU was impenetrable, with no public profile to acknowledge its existence. Its job was to recruit informants at the heart of the IRA and other terrorist groups.

Those who served in or alongside the FRU would rarely be privy to information about fellow operatives or their activities. Similar to the IRA's cell structure, units were small and detached, and for good reason – a captured man could not give away secrets that he did not know, no matter how many body parts may be chopped off.

The HQ of British military intelligence was Templer barracks in Ashford, Kent. It was where all service men or women – army, navy and air force – whose roles made them prone to capture were trained. Bill was resident at Templer on numerous occasions, including one session in 1980 when he underwent highly specialised training as a 'Resistance to Interrogation (RTI)' instructor. That same year, he was promoted to sergeant. Aged 23, it was a notably young age for such rank. He was already a father, with his first son being of school age. Emotionally, Bill was cool and unfazed by his experiences of shootings, bombs and bodies on the streets of Derry and the rolling hills of Tyrone. Commanding officers saw these qualities, and an astute ability at reading people, which marked him out for interrogation training and intelligence gathering.

As an RTI instructor, one of Bill's jobs was to teach soldiers what to do in the event of being taken prisoner by the enemy. During the intense three-month course he became fascinated by the techniques and psychology used by prisoners and their captors.

He recalls: 'It was not all pliers and blowtorches. Every regiment had one such instructor and I got the job for the 16th Regiment (Royal Artillery) which comprised around 800 men. I learned how certain types of people resist interrogation in different ways and how interrogators can give away leads about how best to act towards them. The basic survival technique is that of the "gray man", which is to blend into the background, to become invisible and give the impression that you know little of value. Never be aggressive. Be as helpful as can but while trying not to give anything substantial away. Varying interrogation techniques are used depending on the circumstances of capture.

'A pilot downed behind enemy lines may be treated well and kept alive to be exploited publicly for propaganda purposes. However, a soldier snatched in the heat of battle won't usually be so lucky. His only value to the enemy will be his immediate knowledge of his own side. Once that information is given, he will most likely be killed on the spot because he's no longer of any value. So in that kind of situation you want to convince them that you are still useful in some way.

'In cases like Nairac's, his deep and detailed knowledge makes it likely the IRA would have taken as long as needed to break him down. Other than the chance of a British army unit crashing through the window, they would have probably felt safe enough to do so. In a situation like Northern Ireland, one tactic would be to suggest a willingness to provide future information in exchange for release.

'Sometimes physical torture is used. They'll take off a pinkie, then a thumb next. People tell you what you want to hear if you brutalise them enough, but the best information is gained from inflicting the least amount of pain.

'Messing with your mind through lack of sleep, or doing things like letting you sleep for ten minutes but telling you it's been ten hours, can be very effective. Another tactic is if more than one person is captured, they can be played off against each other.

'Teaching these skills is all about how to react in order to stay alive. Prior to the Troubles, the army only really trained for conventional battlefield capture and interrogation. Northern Ireland presented us with a very different scenario. It ultimately became an intelligence war and we had to learn new tricks both to survive if captured, but also to win the long game.'

'I didn't think that any of this would be of use in future civilian life but it often was. I was trained at getting inside people's heads, being able to read how they worked, why they did certain things, and anticipate their next move. Sometimes in my dealings with Police Scotland, the ulterior motives shone like a beacon. The fact that some of them seemed to think they could treat me like an idiot was also evident. Perhaps they thought they were being clever, but really it was insulting and amateurish.'

The murder of Nairac changed the way the army operated when faced with this new type of guerrilla warfare being fought on its own streets against a largely invisible enemy. There was root and branch reform of structure and techniques. Lessons were truly learned. Bill, never one to take unnecessary risk, learned to become even more astute. The next time Bill returned to Northern Ireland, he would be a ghost. His British Army uniform would stay at home.

17

NICE LASSES

When a soldier comes under fire, the worst thing he can do is lose his composure. Going into a flap serves only to sharply increase his chance of getting killed. One of Bill's Royal Artillery senior officers displayed an ornate plaque of the regimental cannon badge on his office wall, bearing golden letters proclaiming, 'In times of stress the professional soldier must be cool and thoughtful.'

Days after the collapse of the Bill Kidd threat trial, those wise words came back to Bill's mind as he fought to muster self-control. A threat towards his young daughters almost made him lose it. It was the nearest he had come to doing so in a decade.

Bill's two girls, then aged 15 and 18 and living with his former partner, had been for a weekly visit to see their dad. After a traipse through clothes shops and a bite to eat, Bill drove them to Partick train station in his every-day runaround, a Citroen van, and waved them off back home. Bill and Jackie then left Glasgow for an overnight drive to classic car auctions in London.

When Jackie's teenage son got up for school the next morning, he discovered the van, which had been left in the driveway, splattered with paint stripper. Each panel of the vehicle had been daubed with pungent gloop, which had dissolved the white paintwork to expose the bare metal shell. Upon returning home to Anniesland, Bill performed what had become a routine event – inspecting a trashed vehicle and informing police through gritted teeth.

When he flipped over the door of the garage, he saw a sheet of paper that had been pushed through the gap. Typed along the top were the words 'NICE LASSES UV GOT THER'.

In all the years of the criminal vendetta, Bill had remained in control. He had wanted to take direct action after the garage fire but that was over bricks, mortar and cars. This note, however, involved his daughters. In that moment Bill was the closest to taking the law into his own hands: bypassing the police, hunting down his tormentor, and dispatching instant and effective vigilante justice. It was something he could have done readily, as most people click their fingers.

The reference to his girls was craven and creepy. Ominously, the writer may have followed them. Had he watched them shopping, eating or exchanging a farewell hug at the train station? It was clearly meant to get inside Bill's head and it succeeded.

Like a switch being flicked, gone was the astute, smart soldier who had been trained to weigh up every move like a chess player, even in the most testing of circumstances. In its place was the bare-knuckle fighting youth, his teeth clamped in a mask of rage, utterly consumed by a primal desire to maim or kill. In Bill's own candid words, 'I felt like getting hold of a Browning 9mm pistol and putting a round in his chest and two in his head. I was deadly serious.'

He told Jackie, 'Enough is enough, I need to deal with this and it is not going to end well.'

If anything justified a violent response, he argued, it was threats against his daughters. To do nothing would feel like emasculation.

But in 1970s Derry, when faced with bombs, snipers or rioters, to keep a clear head could be the difference between survival and death. On this occasion, had Bill lost control, there would be negligible risk to his own safety, but he would almost certainly have ended up inside a prison cell for many years, convicted of murder or, at the very best, serious assault.

Jackie explained in the most forceful terms that he should not be so stupid and selfish. *Go and get yourself locked up, but then what?* If the vendetta continued and got worse, he would be incarcerated, unable to help his family on the outside. That would be real emasculation.

Not only that, but his imprisonment would give great satisfaction to some police officers, who would be able to say that they had been right all along: he was just a criminal.

It took every ounce of Jackie's persuasive powers to bludgeon sense into Bill's brain and make him realise and accept that he needed to get a grip on his emotions. The reasoning of Jackie – coupled with the words on his regimental sergeant major's office plaque – brought Bill back from the brink and his wild rage gradually abated. To be certain that Bill's apparent calm was not temporary or a bluff, Jackie ordered that they should leave Glasgow and go back to London for a few days to cool off.

The police put an 'urgent response marker' against their home address, which meant that any 999 call would be treated as a priority due to the history of incidents. Bill – who then installed his own CCTV system – was also marked as a 'repeat victim' in the computer system, but the police response remained typically sluggish.

What Bill did not know at the time was that the day before the paint stripper attack on the Citroen and the note about his daughters, John Lawson had been cautioned and interviewed by the CID over the cut hose pipe at his garage site 17 months earlier. Police can only caution a suspect if they have ample evidence. Later, the police would say there was never any evidence against Lawson for this crime and most of the others. This was the second occasion where a crime was committed against Bill the day after police had spoken to Lawson about other crimes. It was becoming a pattern and seemed to be a significant factor towards the commission of some crimes.

It took two months from the 'nice lasses' incident for a pair of uniformed police officers to be dispatched to speak with Lawson at his home in Cadder. He denied having anything to do with the vandalism or the letter and claimed not to know where his accuser lived.

According to the police, Lawson also told them that he had last spoken to Bill in 2008, which was untrue, as he had bought the £150 Ford Transit from him in 2009.

Bill and Jackie provided their fingerprints and DNA samples to allow them to be used for elimination purposes had any been recovered from the threatening letter. The letter was sent to a police laboratory for analysis on 4 October 2011, where it lingered for almost an entire year. When the results came back, they were negative. The writer and deliverer had been careful enough to not leave any marks.

It may have been apparent to senior officers that this was an unusual and serious set of circumstances. Surely the longevity and types of crimes merited the devotion of proper time and effort. Yet the police management stayed idle and aloof as the vendetta escalated. Each of the myriad offences was isolated in its own little bubble and subject to either cursory police attention or none at all.

18

CHRISTMAS GIFT

The stalker shrank low into the car seat and caught his breath when the target came into view. His mouth curled into a satisfied smirk as he watched Bill Johnstone emerge from the end of his street behind the wheel of a sleek vintage Mercedes. Pausing momentarily to see which direction Bill took, he then started his engine and slipped into the flow of traffic. Using the gloom of the December night as a shield, he kept a discreet distance while travelling through the forest of traffic lights at Anniesland Cross, a busy junction of multiple criss-crossing lanes.

Bill's journey was short, less than a mile, and when he parked the SLC coupé in a quiet residential enclave he had no idea he was being watched. The stalker allowed himself another smile and slunk away, knowing he would be back in a few hours to complete his task.

When he returned in the small hours of Monday, 12 December 2011, all was still and the classic gold Mercedes glowed the colour of dark amber under the soft street light. Reaching into his rucksack for a small metal tin of paint stripper, he worked quickly and methodically. The corrosive liquid was doused over the glistening bodywork. From the rucksack came a kitchen knife with a blade of hard, sharp steel which sliced deeply through all four tyres. The noisiest job came last. A heavy lump hammer was swung at each of the car's light clusters and windows, shattering them as easily as a foot cracks an icy puddle.

There was more to do before the sun came up. The stalker made his way to Bill's home, where another vehicle, an imported Toyota Sera with unusual butterfly doors, was parked outside. The paint stripper reappeared from the rucksack and its toxic contents thrown all over the little hatchback coupé.

At nine o'clock that morning, a friend of Bill's came out of his flat to find the destroyed Mercedes.

Bill had moved it to the friend's street because he was going to a classic car auction in London and could not risk leaving such a precious vehicle outside his home. His precaution had been in vain.

The friend circled the broken Mercedes and told Bill it looked like a wild animal was to blame, given the extent of the damage.

When Bill and Jackie returned home two days later, they were not surprised to also see the Toyota's paintwork ruined. The relentless destruction of vehicles was infuriating Bill, costing him a fortune and filling him with paranoia. He and Jackie had become constantly alert to unusual vehicles and people in their street and while driving they scribbled down details of any that might be tailing them. Many people have questioned what would motivate such a prolonged vendetta, which clearly took a great deal of time and effort to perpetrate and sustain. Bill has no simple answers and, frankly, does not possess the inclination nor the expertise to play the role of amateur psychiatrist. But, for what it's worth, he believes that the stalker was deeply humiliated over the van dispute and stung by the subsequent derision and disregard shown towards him. The stalker would surely have bristled indignantly as Bill loudly shared his disdain with mutual associates in the motor trade. Involving the police also seems to have been a trigger. Sometimes seeking simple answers to an illogical situation is futile. How can one understand the reasoning of someone who is unreasonable? Sometimes a neatly defined motive cannot be readily deduced. In the illogical mind of a perpetrator, especially one who operates on the margins of society, it can be completely unfathomable. Maybe it is as simple as thinking 'I'll teach him a lesson.' Who knows? Had Bill backed down quietly, perhaps shown some early contrition over the van dispute, the vendetta would maybe not have continued for so long. Bill regards that theory as wishful thinking. Even if true, he would never back down to bullying and intimidation.

Classic cars which had been bought at auction to be refurbished and sold were constantly moved from place to place, a desperate game of cat and mouse to thwart yet another costly attack. Yet despite the precautions, the wave of vandalism did not stop. On many occasions, the stalker's cunning and patience paid dividends.

Bill had suspected the use of tracking devices on his cars but the large number of attacks suggested that surveillance was also used to sniff out his valuable stock. Following the destruction of his garage in the November 2009 fire, Bill had maintained the Turnberry Motors website as a virtual showroom for his classic cars. It served as a window to attract potential customers but also gave the stalker a hit list of targets, so a year on, in late 2012, Bill had been forced to shut it down, further damaging his business.

Throughout this period any vandalised cars that could not be salvaged were sent to the scrapyard, yielding a nominal sum. Those that were repairable became unprofitable due to the cost of putting them right. New tyres, windows, lights and resprays were not cheap and ate into any profit. The financial cost to Bill was massive.

It seems likely that the stalker had friends who attended the same auctions where Bill was a regular customer. Anyone present could see which vehicles he had bought in these public arenas. Once known, it was a case of finding out where they were stashed.

Another problem was that Bill and Jackie's home was in a cul de sac, with only one way in and out.

Whenever they emerged from their street onto the busy arterial thoroughfare of Great Western Road, they could be seen from numerous vantage points, the most obvious being a pub car park right across the road.

After the attacks on the Mercedes and Toyota, Bill acquired two other stock vehicles – a powerful BMW M3 and a sporty convertible Mercedes SL. Jackie had been using the BMW for a couple of weeks, so it had been occasionally parked at house, but as the Mercedes was new it had only been there since the previous day, 23 December.

On Christmas Eve at 9 p.m., Bill's anxiety persuaded him to shift the vehicles away from the house. Keeping them there would be like giving the stalker a free shot, so he drove them almost two miles to Westbourne Gardens, an affluent and quiet West End street which is home to local celebrities and the wealthy.

After enjoying Christmas festivities with the family, on 27 December Bill returned to Westbourne Gardens, where he discovered an unwelcome present. The Mercedes was destroyed beyond repair. A toxic substance had ruined the paintwork and a blade had turned the soft top into ribbons. A couple of hundred feet away, the BMW was covered in the same corrosive goo. The BMW was a write-off while the Merc generated a costly repair bill.

Again, Bill explained to the police the entire background to the nightmare, which began with the van sale to John Lawson and which had consumed his and Jackie's lives since Turnberry Motors had burned to the ground two years previously. Lawson was spoken to by the police but, as they put it, with 'negative result'.

Again, Jackie told Bill that he could not risk going anywhere near Lawson because it was likely that the consequences of revenge would be extreme – serious injury, death, prison, financial ruin.

To Bill, it felt like being back on the streets of Northern Ireland, where the enemy hid deep in the shadows and never went face-to-face or fought fairly. Sneaky attacks in the dead of night were cowardly but effective and extremely difficult to counter. Unless you ignore the yellow card . . .

In seven months from June to December 2011, seven cars had suffered chemical attacks and other damage. During that time, the stalker had also left his creepy note describing Bill's daughters as 'nice lasses'.

Bill was obliged and expected to follow the rules of engagement, namely to report matters to the police and put faith in the criminal justice system, no matter how inept, or worse, it had continually proven itself to be.

The role of the police bore similarities with Bill's experiences in Northern Ireland four decades earlier. For just as he had regarded some RUC officers as a source of problems and a hindrance, the police in Scotland were clearly working against his interests. They had repeatedly failed to conduct proper investigations, falsely branded him a serial criminal, treated him as a suspect for a crime vendetta being waged against himself and then put him on trial on trumped-up charges of threatening Bill Kidd MSP.

The perpetrator must have begun to nurture delusions of being a master criminal. Little did he know, the police were doing little to catch him. The CID knocked on a few neighbours' doors to ask if they had seen anything. The detectives also concluded that no CCTV had been in the area of either attack – yet the route which Bill drove the Mercedes through Anniesland Cross is well covered by public and private camera systems. Given it was likely he had been followed, why not check them for signs of a pursuer? And so it went on . . . and on. Bill and Jackie's lives consumed by crime and paranoia, 24 hours a day.

19

BAD BLOOD

Volatile, awkward, drunk and obsessed – these were some of the opinions formed by police officers about Bill and Jackie, two innocent victims of a serious, long-running and escalating criminal vendetta that devastated their lives. And in fact most of these police observations could be fairly applied. Bill and Jackie were both capable of volatility, awkwardness and obsession. In their shoes, who wouldn't have been? Bill had been smeared by police as a criminal and pushed to near financial ruin, while Jackie had become suicidal due to the loss of her job, status, SNP friends and familial implosion. For the police to have been the root cause of the couple's high emotions, then use it against them was pretty unsavoury.

The suggestion that they had a problem with alcohol was a cheap shot – insulting and untrue. This seems to have stemmed from the dark moment when Jackie had been suicidal and alone in the hotel room. Having consumed alcohol, and in the depths of despair, she had phoned a female police sergeant to tell her how she felt. Later, the sergeant would provide a formal statement which made reference to Jackie's high emotions and drunkenness, giving the impression it was a common occurrence. To misuse this episode, to exploit Jackie's vulnerability in such a cynical way, was almost as outrageous and wrong as the application of the fake record to Bill.

Since Turnberry Motors and seven classic cars had been destroyed in 2009 the couple had suffered chemical, fire and blade attacks on vehicles belonging to them, had been texted death threats, experienced stalking, and received a razor blade in the post, along with a sinister note about Bill's teenage girls, which almost caused him to lose it.

Prime suspect John Lawson had been occasionally spoken to by police but presumably did not suffer sleepless nights fearing anything other than gentle, occasional chats.

Bill, an engaging, intelligent, personable and reasonable man, has a low tolerance for those who fail him, lie to him or treat him like a fool. While the uniformed police officers who attended the many crime scenes were mostly courteous and professional, there was little they could do other than refer matters to the CID. That's where Bill's problems took root.

In the uniformed ranks, there is a view that some CID officers can think of themselves as a cut above mere beat cops – a high self-opinion usually with little basis to justify it. The CID's response to the garage fire had been lazy and inept. As the crimes mounted up, the CID attitude worsened to become a combination of downright disinterest, misplaced suspicion and naked hostility.

Any idea that complaining to higher-ranked officers would force an improvement in the CID's conduct was wishful thinking. As far as Bill was concerned, these inspectors and superintendents displayed the same level of initiative, resourcefulness and interest in justice as robots. Cosseted by deference and grandiose titles, soothed by the sound of 'Yes, sir' or 'Yes ma'am'.

It seems that the culture of defending officers from

complaints, no matter how poor their conduct or professionalism, remains deeply ingrained. Neither these
senior officers nor the CID were particularly used to the
gruff plain-speaking which they got from Bill. That's not
to concede rudeness on his part, but rather an honesty
and bluntness in response to being dismissed, having his
name smeared, being lied to and patronised by police.

With the arrival of 2012, the vendetta entered its fourth
year and the disdain between Bill and the CID officers of
Maryhill and Partick was potent and mutual. Later this
year, Bill would cross paths with Lawson – an encounter
with near fatal consequences. To the police, this incident
would become a golden opportunity to silence their arch
critic.

The first crime of 2012 came on 28 February, when Bill
received three text messages while standing with friends
in Tennent's Bar, a traditional pub in the West End's Byres
Road area, which buzzes with student life from the nearby
university. The opening salvo stated:

> *prick iv just destroyed your silver merc thinking*
> *about burning it*

Bill immediately called Jackie at home and she checked
the silver Mercedes parked outside: it was unscathed. The
text was a hoax. About 20 minutes later came two more
texts:

> *how much money did you make last year y fat pig*
> *fuck all*

> *wanker your fucked*

Up to this point Bill had chosen not to call numbers which
carried threatening texts, but on this occasion he did so.

He did not expect any meaningful exchange with whom-ever was on the other end, but he knew that a connected call could potentially make it easier for the police to pin-point where the perpetrator was. The call went straight to an answering service.

Bill had by now been designated one police officer, Sergeant Ailie Brown, as a single point of contact due to the large volume of crimes against him. The following day he went to Maryhill, where he reported the messages to Brown, who established that the message came from an unregistered pay-as-you-go mobile. It was not until 27 days later that Brown ordered a check on where and when the number's credit had been last topped up, only getting partial information 16 days after that. The phone's credit had been topped up 20 minutes before the texts were sent. Another 20 days passed before the police learned the top-up had been bought at a newsagent shop on Great Western Road, not far from Bill's home. When they even-tually attended, they were told the CCTV was not working. Broken CCTV aside, the delay was frustrating because had the police acted swiftly they could have spoken to the employee who'd served the customer while their memory was fresh, quite possibly leading to identification. There was little hope of doing so more than two months later. Another unnecessary policing failure.

Bill complained about Brown's delay to the police, which they dealt with by completely ignoring him. He then raised the police's mishandling of his complaint with the Police Investigations and Review Commissioner. They sent it back to the police and told them to respond.

This illustrates Scotland's police complaints system at work – it can be a frustrating and life-sapping process; there is a lack of urgency and it seems designed to deter all but the most patient and determined by burying com-plaints under piles of paper.

Bill finally received an explanation from Police Scotland in December 2016 – almost a full *five years* after the event. A letter from Detective Chief Inspector Andrew Edward said that because the CCTV was not working when the officers checked it, it was 'reasonable to conclude' it was also broken at the time of the transaction. Edward offered no apology for the delay nor did he address Bill's query of the missed opportunity – that a quicker check could have resulted in the shop worker identifying the buyer.

DCI Edward concluded that it was 'regrettable your interactions with the police resulted in you feeling compelled to complain' – which to Bill was a cut-and-paste platitude, cheapened further by the fact it had taken half a decade to make.

At this time, Bill was unaware that Brown, the police officer who he had been told to report to directly, held a negative opinion of himself and Jackie. He only discovered this two years later, when Brown said he was 'very awkward to work with and he had to be on occasion reminded that it was a police operation and not a William Johnstone-led operation, and to that end I had to take matters in hand and explain that fully to Mr Johnstone'.

She added:

> I dealt with Mr Johnstone over a period of around a year and anytime he or his wife complained he would phone, or his wife would email me regularly when she was apparently under the influence of alcohol, threatening suicide. They had a very volatile relationship . . . I used to contact Mr Johnstone to ask him to go and speak with his wife or partner.

When Bill read Brown's statement, which portrayed Jackie as a drunk (this being somehow deduced by the detective from Jackie's single email and calls to others), he was appalled. The implied criticism of Jackie because she had felt suicidal was remarkable, especially in enlightened times of mental health awareness. When Jackie, on the brink of suicide, had emailed the police officer, she could never have imagined that her cry for help would later be turned around and used against her.

Brown went on to dismiss Bill's view of the police not doing enough as 'completely without foundation'. She declared that 'full surveillance' had been put in place at the couple's home address, which sounded impressive until clarified with the admission that 'it was only on one occasion that the surveillance was deployed', adding, 'It is not the case that surveillance was not deployed due to funding issues.'

While the latest text threat investigation was being botched, Bill was contacted by Maryhill detective DC Dan Crilley, who was looking into the incident of the destroyed classic Mercedes five months earlier, just before Christmas 2011. Bill was perplexed when Crilley ordered him to bring his insurance information to their meeting. As Bill sat in the small interview room, the tall figure of Crilley entered with a thick pile of paperwork, which he placed on the table. He sat down with the greeting, 'I hope you've got those insurance documents.' Just as Crilley said this, Bill looked down to see the bogus criminal record atop the pile. He gaped open-mouthed, reached across, grabbed the document and growled, 'What the fuck is that doing here?'

In the 11 months since Bill had discovered the record attached to the Bill Kidd trial citation, he had been verbally assured that the record did not apply to him and the computer record had been put right. Yet there it was, continuing to poison his reputation in the eyes of police officers. Crilley demanded it back, but Bill refused and held it aloft while continuing to demand answers.

The stand-off ended when Brown walked into the tiny

room and saw the offending documents in Bill's upraised hand. She hauled her flustered colleague from the room, presumably to explain the story of the bogus record, and when they returned Crilley suggested to Bill that they should start the meeting afresh.

'No, we won't start again,' Bill replied. 'We'll start where we left off. Where did you get that record and why is it still attached to my name a year after I was told it had been removed?'

The officers could not offer any sensible or acceptable answers. Did this explain Crilley's cool demeanour and odd demand for insurance documents? Had he spent five months thinking he was dealing with Bill Johnstone, serial *criminal*, not Bill Johnstone, serial *victim*, and that the destroyed Mercedes was some kind of insurance scam perpetrated by himself?

Bill let rip at the pair and told them that he had made no insurance claims because to do so would have made him uninsurable. He explained that his lost garage, plus 18 damaged or ruined vehicles, had cost him hundreds of thousands of pounds and that, despite the vast amount of evidence and leads available to the CID, no one had been brought to justice.

The heated exchange was nothing compared to what followed two weeks later when Bill returned to Maryhill to report yet more crimes. Late at night on 15 April, Jackie's teenage son had been in his bedroom when a neighbour banged loudly on the front door. Bill's white Citroen van – the one that had previously been daubed in paint stripper – was engulfed in flames. A Jaguar beside it suffered heat damage to its bumper while a Rover, a stock vehicle, had been smeared with a corrosive substance. The van was a write-off.

Bill was glad of Jackie's presence when he attended Maryhill to give a statement about the latest attack because

Above.
Bill Johnstone stands at the derelict site of Turnberry Motors, which was destroyed by fire in 2009. (Les Gallagher)

Left.
Odd job man and former garage customer John Lawson, who disputed his purchase of a white van with Bill.

Above.
A teenage Bill (front left) apparently destined for a life as a merchant seaman at the Prince of Wales Sea Training School in Dover, where he became 'leading boy'.

Right.
Teenage soldier William 'Buff' Miller on patrol in Derry's Bogside in 1976 before he was shot dead by a sniper.

Bill taking a break while on patrol in Northern Ireland in 1979 at the height of The Troubles.

Beaming with happiness on the night of his election to the Scottish Parliament in 2007, the SNP's Bill Kidd and his election agent, Jackie Mills.

In happier times during a 2003 trip to New York, Sandra White MSP (far left) beside Liz Quinn, with a family friend and Liz's daughter, Jackie Mills (far right).

Bill and Jackie leaving Glasgow Sheriff Court. Relieved at his acquittal by a jury, Bill knew that his long fight for justice was not over. (Les Gallagher)

had she not been there, he believes he could have ended up in a cell.

The officer taking the statement from Bill was DS David Patrick, who was handed a pile of paperwork by Brown just as they all sat down. After what had just happened with Crilley, Bill began with the request for an assurance that the bogus record was not tucked away somewhere within the documents. Patrick seemed unimpressed and the sour tone in the room escalated into a shouting match. Bill denounced the multiple police failures and smears. Another officer pointed to the exit with the comment, 'If you don't like what you're getting, there's the door.'

Bill stormed into the corridor, where the commotion attracted the attention of DI Stephen Healy, who suggested they should all enter his office. Bill was unfazed by the rank of those he spoke to and admits that in the extreme situation he found himself in he was sometimes brusque. Bill began by challenging Healy about what he was doing about the multiple crimes he and Jackie had suffered.

By this stage, Bill believes that some higher ranking police officers had realised that the situation with CID had spiralled out of control. One of the officers chimed in with the advice that Bill should continue to report any new crimes because, eventually, the perpetrator would inevitably make a mistake.

Bill recalls: 'I was not interested in any more patronising rubbish. The suggestion that I should just go away quietly and sit back for even more crimes to happen, then put my faith in the police, was unbelievable. The irony was that the person responsible for the crimes had already made mistakes but had evaded arrest because of the police's countless mistakes and acts of laziness. Lawson couldn't get caught if he had been trying. Healy said there was no evidence against him, to which I responded, "I'm the motor trader, I sell cars. You're the cop, you get evidence."

'I'd been in the station more times than the officers who worked there. Everyone knew that the CID had repeatedly failed to conduct basic enquiries and that I was given a fake criminal record which saw me being treated like a scumbag.'

Two days after the latest fire attack, Bill received three text messages.

The first stated:

> *VAN ROVER AND JAG FUCKED. NEXT IT A*
> *HAMMER OVER THE BACK OF YOUR HEID*
> *WHEN YOU WALK OUT 3 JUDGES [a pub*
> *frequented by Bill] HA HA YOU FINISHED.*

These threats, again from pay-as-you-go throwaways, were reported to the police. Officers duly spoke to Lawson but closed the case with the conclusion: 'There is no evidence linking the suspect to this crime other than the complainer's suspicions.'

Two years later, DS Patrick provided an alternative take on Bill's attendance at Maryhill that day. Rather than being there to give a statement about the Citroen fire, according to Patrick, Bill was 'wanting to remonstrate about a long running series of vandalisms and communications act offences allegedly committed by John Lawson'.

Patrick used the word 'feud' to describe the relationship between Bill and Lawson. This word can be cynically deployed in cases where an innocent person is subject to multiple crimes. By describing a one-way vendetta as a feud is to falsely suggest the criminality is two way and tit-for-tat, thereby diminishing any sympathy for the victim by applying equal guilt to one as the other.

The word suggested that Bill had avenged the crimes. It was a dangerous misuse of language. But over the years of the vendetta, the toxic word found its way into the mountain of crime reports, statements, emails and letters generated by police. As well as implying Bill's guilt, 'feud' also served to confirm that Lawson was a guilty party too – which was at odds with the police's claim that there was no evidence of such.

Patrick went on to describe Bill and Jackie as 'very unreasonable individuals who appeared to have an obsession with John Lawson'. The description of Bill as unreasonable set his teeth on edge. What was unreasonable about a basic expectation of sound policing; about responding robustly to innumerable failures and being falsely traduced as a violent and dishonest man?

Despite the police's view of Bill as obsessed and their contention of no evidence against Lawson, they were about to pay the prime suspect another visit. More mistakes would follow.

20

TEXT TERROR

John Lawson opened his front door to a pair of CID detectives investigating the fire that destroyed Bill's Citroen van outside his house. Lawson agreed to let in DS Alex Cameron and DC John Wallace but they could do little more than perform a cursory poke around because of the large volume of clutter hoarded inside his small flat.

They then did the same inside two nearby lock-up garages rented by Lawson, where they found petrol, apparently to fuel a welding machine, and a bottle of flammable paint thinner, which they confiscated with a view to having it analysed, although this was never done. Lawson was then given a warning by the police about committing 'illegal acts' against Bill. To Bill's disbelief, disquiet and disgust, he then received a similar warning in a phone call from DS Cameron.

Bill recalled: 'Cameron phoned and said he'd spoken to Lawson and that he was going to say the same thing to me. I could hardly believe what followed – he said that he was warning me as well. It was outrageous and offensive. Yet again, I was being treated like a criminal and the police were determined to portray it as a "feud". I got angry and asked Cameron if he still had the bogus criminal record in front of him and told him that instead of lecturing me he should do his job properly.'

The day after the police visit to Lawson's flat, Bill suffered another vehicle attack, with paint stripper splashed over a classic Mercedes. Hours later, he received 11 menacing text messages.

This was the third occasion in which crimes were inflicted against Bill the day after Lawson had been spoken to by police. Not that the police seemed to regard this pattern as suspicious.

Even by the dismal standards experienced in the two and a half years since the garage blaze, the collective CID response to these two new crimes was not just laughably incompetent but dangerously negligent.

The latest car targeted was a Mercedes SL320, which Bill had parked away from the house in a vain attempt at protecting it. The blue paintwork was coated with a viscous chemical that caused the gleaming surface to bubble and blister.

Bill greeted a female sergeant at the scene in the upmarket West End area of Park, which contains a mix of commercial and residential townhouses perched grandly above Kelvingrove Park. The car was parked outside a finance company, where a 29-year-old female employee told police it was unscathed when she arrived at 5 a.m. and when she popped out at 6.30 a.m., but it had been damaged when she went out to feed a parking meter at 10 a.m.

This witness's precise timings provided a useful three-and-a-half-hour window in which the attack took place. Bill pointed out two domed CCTV cameras fixed to the front of the finance company's office, which covered the pavement although not the car itself. Company management told the CID officers they did not possess the technical ability to burn the footage onto a disc straight away but that it could be arranged. Three days later – on 14 May

– the company emailed the police to say the footage was available but was only kept for seven days and copying it would incur a small administrative fee from their security provider.

Bill chased up the CID officers to see whether they had got the footage and reminded them that the clock was ticking; they only had a few days to get it. It wasn't until 21 May – ten days after the crime – that Reid returned to the finance company to retrieve the CCTV recording. Too late. It had been automatically wiped. Reid's excuse was that during the crucial period she had been working night shifts and had days off. She had asked a day shift colleague to retrieve it, but they had failed to do so. Their excuse was that Reid had not briefed them properly, by not providing a description of any suspect they were supposed to be looking for, nor any information about the time period that should be viewed.

Bill complained about this latest missed opportunity. It took *four years* of negotiating the ponderous police complaints labyrinth for failure to be admitted. In May 2015, Detective Chief Inspector Andrew Edward upheld Bill's complaint, which he described as an 'irregularity in procedure', but offered no apology and said that no action would be taken against any officer. It was another 16 months before Edward said sorry and only after being told by the Police Investigations and Review Commissioner that his original response was not good enough.

Edward finally stated: 'It is the case the CCTV should have been recovered by Police Scotland, and I offer my apologies to you for this failing.'

Another strange aspect of the Mercedes attack was information from the same female witness who saw a man 'wipe' the car after she noted the damage at 10 a.m. Her sighting occurred during the two-hour period before Bill got there. When Bill learned about this years later, he questioned why no effort had been given to identify the mystery man.

The explanation offered by the police to PIRC was that they had not pursued it because the man matched Bill's description. The claim stank. Given that a credible witness potentially put Bill at the scene two hours *before* the time he stated, then why not challenge him about it at the time?

As Bill put it: 'If the police genuinely thought that I'd lied about what time I was there, that it was me wiping the car, then they would have been all over me. The truth is this man may have been the attacker – and may also have been captured on the lost CCTV – but the police failed to follow the lead and only came up with their nonsense excuse after I found out about it, complained they'd done nothing and when PIRC demanded answers. PIRC just swallowed this nonsense.'

Hours after trashing the Mercedes, Bill's stalker was in a gloating mood. Within a 13-minute period that afternoon, Bill received 11 text messages from an unrecognised number. The messages were all in block capital letters and riddled with poor grammar and misspellings and left little doubt about the sender's mindset.

15.32   *THATS A NICE DARK LANE DOWN TO YOUR NEW FLAT! SOON VERY SOON!*

15.33   *THATS WHAT HAPPENS WHEN YOUR A PEADO! UR DIRTY SCUM*

15.34   *YOU LIKE THOSE OLD MERCEDES DONT U! SO DO WE! HA HA*

15.36   *YOU BETTER HAVE FIRE INSURANCE SORTED! THE FIRE ENGINES CANT GET DOWN THAT LANE BECAUSE THE SCAFFOLD!*

15.38   *YOUR STUPID WIFE LEAD US RIGHT TO
         YOU!*

15.38   *WHAT DOES IT FEEL LIKE TO BE
         DESTROYED?*

15.40   *YOU GOING TO THREE JUDGES
         TONIGHT? OR ARE YOU CLEANING UP
         YOUR OLD MERCEDES?*

15.41   *WE HAVE STOOD BESIDE YOU ON THE
         TRAIN. WHERES YOUR STUPID BEARD?
         NOT LONG NOW!*

15.42   *YOUVE BEEN TOLD TO GET OUT OF
         GLASGOW. LAST WARNING OR YOUR
         NEW HOUSE GETS IT LIKE YOUR
         GARAGE!*

15.43   *HOW MUCH HAVE YOU LOST NOW?*

15.45   *IS THE POLICE OM YOUR FRIENDS AND
         FAMILY?*

The third and seventh texts were brazen confessions of
the sender being responsible for wrecking the Mercedes
that morning. The first message referred to a flat which
Bill owned in the Park area, while the fourth threatened
to set fire to it.

The fifth and eighth – referring to Jackie as Bill's 'stupid wife' and to standing beside him on a train – were
evidence of them being stalked while going about their
daily lives.

The final 'friends and family' message suggested the
sender knew Bill had been in frequent contact with the
police. Perhaps someone like John Lawson, who was questioned the day before for what was, as far as Bill knew, not
the first time.

By far the most damning and revelatory of the texts was the ninth, which threatened to set fire to Bill's house 'like your garage'.

Sergeant Andy Gibson was tasked with taking Bill's statement about the latest text messages and transcribing every single letter, exactly as they appeared on the screen. When he reached the ninth text about the garage fire, the police officer's pen paused and remained still in his unsure hand while his eyes rose up to meet Bill's gaze.

At the time of the Turnberry Road blaze, the police had claimed there were 'no suspicious circumstances', a false proclamation, given their lack of investigation. Bill's determined campaign for the truth had forced them to back down and eventually concede 'the cause of the fire was unknown'. And yet now – staring them in the face – was an admission that not only was the fire a deliberate criminal act but it could be tied to the most recent crime in a long and dirty vendetta.

The ninth text could have been written in neon letters ten feet high. It presented the police with either a big problem, or a game-changing opportunity, depending on how they chose to view it.

Maybe a senior officer would be brave enough to take the honest but difficult decision to do the right thing, to dispense with game-playing and obfuscation. Perhaps Bill would now be treated with respect, as a hard-working ex-army officer who was a serial victim of crime not a serial criminal.

Wipe the slate clean. Maybe the CID would discover a hunger to chase leads without prejudice, to gather evidence for prosecutors to bring the stalker to justice.

Not only did the 11 messages tie the garage fire to the entire vendetta, they also contained threats to set fire to Bill's home, which could claim lives. Given the history of fire-raising, the threat could not be taken lightly.

Would these text messages be a catalyst for change or had the catalogue of failures become so bad that it was too late for the police to put them right? Would the instinct to cover-up, to ignore difficult truths and to protect each other, prevail?

The only choice should have been for the police to allocate resources necessary to tackle the nightmare that had consumed the lives of Bill and Jackie. But Bill does not believe in fairy stories. He had no doubt that they could not back down; they were entrenched, neutered by their own misdeeds and mistakes, cemented with stubborn pride.

Despite the damning text message, still no crime report was ever raised for the garage fire.

And despite the seriousness of the messages, the CID did not instigate any check on the number from which they came until 29 May – 18 days after the crimes took place.

It is not too much of a stretch to believe the cursory check only happened – yet again – because their hand was forced. Bill's lawyer Chris Rogers faxed a letter of complaint to the police's professional standards unit, complaining of inaction, and on the same day they ordered the checks to be made.

On 10 June, the police were told, unsurprisingly, that the 11 texts were from an unregistered pay-as-you-go number. It took another two months for the police to learn it had been topped up with £10 of credit at 3.28 p.m. on 11 April – four minutes before the first text was sent.

The credit was bought at Anniesland News, a shop a short distance from Bill and Jackie's home. What followed was perhaps more cock-up than conspiracy. The police mistakenly attended *another* newsagent shop, RS McColl, which is across the street from Anniesland News, and enquired about CCTV. More than a month passed before someone realised they'd gone into the wrong shop. By the time they pitched up at Anniesland News they were told the CCTV was wiped after 30 days. This was now almost six months after the event.

Further checks on the number yielded nothing; the CID hit a dead end and the crime report was filed, marked 'unsolved'. Along with all the rest of them.

21

HAT-TRICK

Surveying the costly destruction of three more cars, Bill tried to keep his cool at the CID officer's line of questioning. It was August 2012 and Bill was seething. A Subaru, a Mercedes and an Audi – stashed in a quiet suburban street – had all been destroyed.

'So Mr Johnstone, what makes you believe it was paint stripper?'

'Can you tell me again why exactly you left these cars here?'

'Why do you think a knife was used on the tyres?'

Detective Constable John Wallace's questions and tone, loaded with implied guilt, caused Bill's anger to boil over.

Standing in a Bearsden avenue of post-war bungalows and twitching net curtains, Bill angrily retorted to DC Wallace's question, 'Do you think he stabbed the tyres with his dick?'

He had lost count of how many vehicles had been damaged or destroyed, but it was now more than twenty. The financial cost was incalculable. The cat-and-mouse game of hiding cars was draining. Worse than being the victim of a criminal vendetta was having his life paralysed and consumed by the Kafkaesque experience of police hostility, inaction and mistakes. With hindsight, the language used in response to DC Wallace could have been more measured, but even a saint might have snapped under such prolonged and extraordinary pressure.

When Bill went to Maryhill police station to report the hat-trick of destruction in Bearsden, he initially spoke to Detective Inspector Stephen Healy, whom he had previously clashed with over a paper copy of the criminal record in his file long after its supposed deletion.

Bill's heart sank when he saw through a glass partition DC Wallace in conversation with DI Healy.

Bill recalls: 'I've no idea what they were speaking about, but these were the same officers who I had already had problems with and were subject to an ongoing professional standards complaint. When Wallace asked me why I thought it was paint stripper that had been used, I told him it was because the paint was falling off the cars and I know what paint stripper is. I also reminded him that it had been happening for years.

'Healy also asked about whether the cars were insured. The questions were absurd. You didn't need to understand interrogation techniques to realise what was going on. From the tone of the questions and the way they were angled, I was being viewed with suspicion. Who knows, maybe the fake criminal record was still having an influence?

'When I told Wallace that I thought he was an amateur and that I could do a better job myself, his face turned red. If he was angry, then it was nothing like how I felt.

'I told them that they should be doing something about John Lawson, who was a knife carrier, because eventually someone was going to get hurt.'

For around a week, the black Mercedes and bottle green Audi had been safely stowed in a quiet residential backwater two miles north of Bill and Jackie's home. Bill had spent a few days driving the third car, a Subaru

Outback, which he then decided to park in the same place. Bill suspects that he was tailed. When he returned the next morning, the first day of August 2012, each of the cars had been methodically trashed. All six kerbside tyres had been slashed; every single panel, including their boots and bonnets, had been scored with a sharp object and daubed with corrosive liquid. They were fit only for scrap.

It is not as if DC Wallace was unaware of the background to this recent crime. He had been involved in the investigation three months earlier, when Bill's Citroen van had been torched outside his home. What stuck in Bill's mind about the police's handling of that episode was Wallace's colleague, DS Alex Cameron, issuing warnings to both himself and Lawson, perpetuating the falsehood of a two-way feud rather than a one-way vendetta. Another memorable and jarring aspect was that the day after the detectives spoke to Lawson about the Citroen fire, yet another car had been trashed and Bill had received the 11 threatening text messages.

Bill left DC Wallace and his colleague, Suzanne Walker, to knock on doors to see if any of the residents had seen anything suspicious, while he phoned a friend in the motor trade to transport the ruined cars to his Lanarkshire yard, where four of Bill's damaged vehicles were already in storage. Later that day, Bill got a call from his old friend, who was puzzled by his dealing with the police.

Bill recalled: 'When he was loading the cars onto the transporter, the police began asking him questions about how I had been behaving and they also wanted to know what I had said when I phoned him. He said to me, "Bill, do these cops think you're doing your own motors?" Knowing what I had been through, he was surprised and bemused by it.'

Reporting the latest attack to police yet again felt like

going through the motions. It could not be any clearer to Bill that the police were not merely disinterested but antagonistic. While his complaints over the previous three years were justified, they had also contributed towards the poisonous relationship that now existed. The police do not like being complained about.

He was also sure that despite assurances from high-ranking officers that the fake criminal record had been excised and disregarded, its toxic legacy continued to influence police conduct, most of all within the ranks of CID.

The abrasive verbal spat with DC Wallace took place at 1.45 p.m. The exact words spoken by Bill would become of major significance – potentially the difference between exoneration and freedom or financial ruin and a long spell of imprisonment.

Less than eight hours afterwards, the vendetta would take a dramatic turn with an unexpected street encounter between Bill and the man he blamed for the criminal campaign. This time, it would not be cars getting damaged.

22

THE ARMY: SHADOWLANDS

When Bill was sent back across the Irish Sea in 1980, he had long scruffy hair, a beard and wore a battered leather jacket. On the inside, his DNA was 100 per cent military, a combination of natural aptitude, extensive training and invaluable experience. While regular British soldiers in uniform and insignia patrolled hot spots such as Derry's Bogside, Bill operated deep in the shadows.

Officially he was a 23-year-old Royal Artillery sergeant. But in fact his role as a 'resistance to interrogation' instructor, having risen quickly from regimental, through brigade and now into divisional intelligence, meant he was the eyes and ears of the army, covering the whole of Northern Ireland. It was not a job for the faint-hearted.

Bill worked intimately with the British Army's FRU and occasionally crossed paths with 14 Int, also known as 'The Det', and which fulfilled the same intelligence-gathering role for the SAS and other special forces. If anything, the ghostlike FRU was even more opaque than the special forces unit, whose tactics were sometimes viewed as being overly aggressive.

Based in Girdwood Park barracks in Belfast, their

everyday vehicles were nondescript VW Passats, Citroens and the like. The two-man teams were heavily armed. Bill carried a Browning 9mm handgun, while a light machine gun was within grabbing distance in the car's footwell. Sometimes there would also be a Winchester pump-action shotgun with special issue military ammunition that could 'stop a car in its tracks and cut a person in half', according to Bill.

Those who skulked undercover, in the darkest sphere of the dirty war, were acutely aware of the risks. But three years after Captain Robert Nairac's torture and murder by the IRA, as the death toll on all sides climbed ever upwards, Bill rarely dwelt on his fate in the event of being compromised: torture, execution, unmarked grave, posthumous medal. Best not to think too much about it.

One FRU man spent three years running a video rental shop in Tyrone. An ill-judged romantic dalliance led to his cover being blown and he was instantly magicked out by the military, never to return. Others worked as taxi drivers or barmen, deep undercover. An ordinary employment agency in the UK mainland served as an unwitting tool of military intelligence. FRU and 14 Int operatives were sent over to work in Northern Ireland as labourers. With bogus credentials and long hair, the rough-and-ready young men from places like Glasgow, Manchester and Newcastle had no whiff of army. While getting their hands dirty on building sites, these fake civvies were spying on the activities of Republican and Loyalist terror networks.

In *The Day of the Jackal*, the classic 1971 novel by Frederick Forsyth, a hitman acquires a British passport by stealing the name and date of birth of a dead child. According to Bill, the same method was used by army intelligence in Northern Ireland. The passport holder was never likely to be unmasked by the IRA.

Intelligence work required Bill to 'get eyes' on major

players who had blood on their hands but rarely spilled it personally. The terror mastermind could be the outwardly respectable small-town estate agent or ruddy-faced smiling farmer. Discreetly taken photos were acquired of targets as they went about their routine business. Bill never went on an aimless drive out of curiosity. There was a clear purpose to every single action, with each factor carefully weighed lest complacency lead him into a fatal trap.

Bill's height of around five foot eight was a useful attribute while trying to be a 'grey man', unnoticed by locals who were sharply attuned to anything out of the ordinary, especially strange faces. A Sandhurst six-footer would stick out like a sore thumb. His ragged, unfashionable clothing added another layer of anonymity. No natty threads or sharp haircuts in Bogside, an urban enclave little different to the Easterhouse of Bill's youth. Slightly problematic to blending in was his prime physical condition, akin to a professional boxer, which he did his best to disguise beneath outsized clothing.

On occasions, Bill would ditch the rags and don the uniform of other regiments to join them on patrol. One day he might be an Argyll & Sutherland Highlander, the next a Royal Green Jacket.

These regiments gathered their own street level intelligence, which was fed upwards to others, and they also received a downward flow of information from those who had sight of the bigger picture. While out on these patrols, Bill would liaise with section commanders. Often all that was needed was a crucial nod of the head towards a car, a place or a face of particular interest to the patrolling regiment.

Formal introductions were rare. Just as Nairac had informally approached Bill on a Derry rooftop four years prior, very few people needed to know who Bill was, nor did he expect to be told the names of others involved in their murky world. During one low-flying helicopter trip to Cookstown, he recalls being accompanied by 'a pile of other shady characters', none of whom made eye contact, let alone small talk. Bill learned to keep his mouth shut and his eyes and ears wide open.

While most of the job was about waiting and watching, there were occasions where meeting informants was necessary. A clandestine rendezvous at 3 a.m. between British army intelligence officers and an IRA mole epitomised the paranoia enveloping Northern Ireland at that time, with trust being the rarest commodity. Informants were categorised on the measure of how reliable, valuable and prolific they were. Category A informants were those whose information was mostly accurate and high-level, the kind that foiled bomb plots and prevented innocent people from being blown to bits.

But informants did not grow on trees. Decent people who wanted to stem the bloodshed could sometimes be persuaded. When a carrot was not enough to turn someone, a stick would often give them no choice but to betray their own families, friends and communities and work for the hated Brits.

For example, a civilian quarry worker suspected of pilfering explosives under IRA duress would be pulled in and told that he was looking at 30 years in prison. There was evidence, he was told. Whether or not this was an empty threat did not matter. The result, one newly minted Category A informant. Once signed up, there was no way back. The power held over informants was the knowledge that if their secret became known, they would be murdered and their families shamed by association with a 'grass'. Summary executions of suspected traitors were commonplace. Bill had previously pulled a suspected IRA man's corpse from a wheelie bin. There were no appeals in paramilitary kangaroo courts.

The army became adept at exploiting human frailties. As Bill puts it, 'People are people.' Discovering someone's weak points, whether sex or money, made them susceptible to a tap on the shoulder and not-so-gentle persuasion. A person who has a grudge or is riven with jealousy towards someone who happens to be a member of a terrorist group may seek comfort by whispering anonymous tips about them down the phone. Once the army worked out the caller's identity, and they often did, they then had no choice but sign on the dotted line as an employee – for life – of Her Majesty. After all, what would happen if news of their sneaky phone calls ever reached the wrong ears?

Another tactic used by the army was to very publicly snatch a suspect from the heart of staunch Republican territory, only to then release them out the back door of the barracks quickly afterwards. The jungle drums would beat. Why were they let out so soon? Did they talk? What did they say? With paranoia prevalent, this simple stunt could be enough to place a permanent question mark over the hapless arrestee. He did not dwell on the morals of his role – to him, it was pretty simple: he was there to counter the tide of bloodletting. He was a peacemaker. To aspire to some ideal of fair play was not just naive but dangerous. It was a war, not a sporting contest, although he wanted nothing to do with some of the more extreme methods.

Throughout the early 1980s, Bill would slink in and out of Northern Ireland, sometimes spending a few days, weeks or months there at a time. There was never any pattern to his movements, either arriving in the dead of night by military helicopter or behind the wheel of a civilian car on a ferry from Liverpool or Stranraer.

When commanding officers thought it wise for Bill to take a step back from the action, they found him a day job at Glasgow's Queen Street and Dumbarton recruiting offices – which tickled him, having walked in as a teenage merchant seaman after his old school pal told him to 'fuck that navy shite'. Much as some police officers at the fag end of their careers find themselves sitting around a court all day, recruitment is often a job for those in the twilight of their career and who are, putting it politely, no longer fighting fit. When Bill appeared in the office, his puzzled colleagues wondered what on earth he was doing there, but they knew not to ask.

Intelligence missions in Northern Ireland were punctuated by spells of training soldiers how to deal with the nightmare scenario of capture and interrogation. He served as an instructor to Territorial Army SAS troops in Port Glasgow and the Royal Artillery in Glasgow's West End. The part-timers were not always appreciative of Bill's robust methods and manner, but it was a deadly serious business and he made no apologies.

When Argentina invaded the Falkland Islands in 1982 and a British task force was deployed in response, there was no curtailment to the violence in Northern Ireland, where there were still 110 recorded deaths that year. As the brief and bloody conflict raged in the frozen South Atlantic, Bill's skills and knowledge were considered to be of much greater value in Northern Ireland, although he would later be dispatched to the Falklands.

Violence and terror had a corrosive effect on the rule of law and Northern Ireland's justice system became tainted. The Royal Ulster Constabulary (RUC), the largely Protestant police force, did not have the authority to enforce the law in many Catholic communities where they were reviled. Bill and his army colleagues referred to the RUC as 'rent a riot', as their presence on the streets was enough to bring out masked youths, snipers, petrol bombs and bricks. Bill worked alongside many brave and honest uniformed RUC men. Yes, some were influenced by religious bigotry which fed a vicious circle of mutual mistrust with Catholics, but others were solid and decent.

Moving into intelligence, Bill began to see an even darker side to the RUC, viewing its Special Branch with distrust. Boorish bigotry was one thing but corruption and collusion with Loyalist terrorists was quite another. Some detectives thought nothing of blatantly fitting up Catholics. Falsifying and planting evidence was commonplace. They were guilty of something, went the rationale.

Decades later, it is widely accepted that there were extraordinary and unjustifiable acts of collusion between Loyalist murder gangs, some in the RUC and rogue sections of the military. Secrets were whispered into the ears of the Loyalist death squads, who would then pull a trigger or plant a bomb. Many incidents of police and military shoot-to-kill – unlawfully gunning down suspected IRA members – are also now proven.

'When we were out on the streets with the RUC boys in uniform, they were mostly just like us, trying to do a job,' Bill said. 'They used to warn us about their own bosses, telling us to be careful about what we said to the bastards in suits because they couldn't be trusted. When I moved into intelligence, I saw it first hand. Too many of the RUC hierarchy, the so-called bastards in suits, were infiltrated and compromised by Loyalists. As a result we told them absolutely nothing of real value.'

23

DAGGER DRAWN

The double-edged dagger sliced, cut and nicked John Lawson, causing five separate wounds to his upper body. There was plenty of blood and lots of noise, some of the scarring was permanent, but his life was not in danger. Bill was mostly unscathed from the fight, which had been brief but bloody. He dialled 999 and calmly informed the operator what had happened while keeping his foot on top of the sticky blade, waiting for blue lights to fill the tree-lined lane in Glasgow's West End.

Following the discovery of the three destroyed cars in Bearsden earlier in the day, Bill and Jackie had decided to go for a drink that Wednesday night. As Jackie drove past the Rock pub, out the corner of his eye Bill caught a glimpse of Lawson, ducking up a side road. Bill yelled at Jackie to stop. He had stashed a Volvo car in the same area and feared that Lawson was on a mission.

Enough was enough.

Bill sprang from the passenger seat and followed on foot, cutting up Hyndland Road onto Crown Road South, a narrow residential street underneath a canopy of verdant summer foliage. After around a hundred metres he was startled when he almost walked straight into Lawson, who had turned and stopped at the sound of quickly approaching footsteps. Lawson was poised between two sandstone pillars at the entrance to Crown Terrace, an elevated Georgian street, the type which excites estate agents on nearby Byres Road. It is not an address that usually hosts knife fights.

Lawson later told police that Bill produced the weapon. According to Bill, it was Lawson who had it, poking from a white plastic bag, and that he shouted, 'I've done your garage and motors. If you don't get tae fuck I'll tan you an' all.' The truth of these and other contrary claims would be for a jury to decide at a later date.

More than three years had passed since Lawson bought the Transit van from Bill. Much had happened since: a business had been burned to the ground; dozens of cars had been damaged or destroyed by fire, blades and paint strippcr; innumerable text threats had been received; acts of stalking had been noted; a razor blade had been sent in the post; and sinister taunts towards Bill's teenage daughters had been made. And here they both were, face-to-face and completely alone. No witnesses, only the swish of branches in the mild August breeze and the distant hum of evening traffic.

At any point during the criminal vendetta, Bill could have taken vigilante action. There were times where he had come to the very brink, especially when his children were being dragged into it, but he always remained disciplined enough to take a step back – partly due to his military training, but often helped by Jackie's calming intervention.

The distance between the two men shortened and confrontation turned to action. They grappled, then toppled over a low wall and landed in the undergrowth. In the frenzy, the six-inch knife caught Lawson on his arms, back and chest. The worst cut needed six stitches, while another needed three. On the Glasgow Coma Scale, a measure of consciousness devised by Glasgow neurologists in the 1970s, he later scored the highest reading of 15 while being treated by A&E medics, denoting full alertness.

Bill kicked the knife into the road and Lawson scrambled away, trailing splashes of red. He reached a nearby flat and buzzed the intercom but the cautious resident, a retired university lecturer in her seventies, refused to allow access to the communal close. Having heard the shouts and screams, she dialled 999, but Bill had already done so, keeping his eyes trained on Lawson while telling the emergency operator about the knife being pulled on him and urging them to send police and an ambulance.

Jackie's nerves were shot. Having driven in the direction Bill had taken, she saw Lawson with a white plastic bag in his right hand. By the time she was able to park the car and return on foot, it was all over. She saw the bloody knife, its handle still covered by a bag, and moved it to the edge of the road to prevent vehicles from driving over it.

When unformed officers arrived, they busied themselves with preserving the scene and ensuring that no possible witnesses attempted to leave. Bill explained to the constables what had happened, but when he later retold the story to the CID he sensed they were not much interested in his version of events or, as he puts it, 'My fate was already sealed – they had me guilty almost as soon as Lawson hit the deck.'

Bill was handcuffed and driven to Stewart Street police station, where he was locked in a cell and ordered to put on paper overalls so that his clothing could undergo forensic examination. Detective Sergeant David Patrick was assigned the 'reporting officer', whose duty was to submit the case to the Crown Office, where lawyers would then decide the strength of the case. Bill had crossed paths with DS Patrick before, as he had also been the reporting officer for the Citroen van fire a few months prior. Bill was barefoot and suspicious when he received a cell visit from DS Patrick. The detective began by asking to see Bill's injuries, which amounted to a few cuts and grazes.

Bill explained to the detective that Lawson was the aggressor, which was met by an assurance that a thorough investigation would take place. Crucially, Bill knew how important tests on the knife could prove to be and urged DS Patrick to be thorough. Hours later, at around 3.30 a.m., Bill was charged with stabbing Lawson.

The haste with which this happened was of grave concern. Bill was immediately fearful of some in the CID who held an apparently blinkered determination to disregard, even suppress, the extensive background to the saga. A stabbing conviction and lengthy jail sentence would decisively eliminate the problem of Bill's tiresome complaints against the police. Who would listen to the bleating of a jailed thug who took a knife to someone?

The police's blindness continued, even becoming more entrenched, as the case disappeared into the black hole of Scotland's criminal justice system. A catalogue of other strange and concerning things happened – or did not happen. Despite the diametrically opposing claims by both men about who the knife belonged to, the police decided not to subject it to DNA or fingerprint testing. So much for being thorough. Bill and his lawyers believe such tests could have presented the police and Crown with a very different picture.

Two mobile phones, a phone SIM card and a diary were seized from Lawson by police on the night of the incident. Over the following two years, Bill's lawyers requested that the items be examined in the hope they could yield evidence in relation to the knife attack and the other crimes. The police took the position, contrary to their own records, that no phones or other items had been recovered from Lawson and that reference to them in their paperwork was down to an admin error. After prolonged pressure from Bill's lawyer, the police changed their story and submitted one of Lawson's supposedly non-existent phones for analysis. Unfortunately, they explained, the other items had been returned to Lawson, as they were new, therefore not likely to give any evidence. Years later, there was no way to verify the final version of the police's shifting position.

The street clash happened on the evening of 1 August 2012 and Lawson was discharged from hospital the following day, while Bill spent a second night in the city centre police cell.

When Lawson left hospital, he called a private hire taxi for a lift home. By coincidence, Bill knew the driver's brother, who later told him that Lawson had been protective of the mobile number he had used and urged the driver not to share it with anyone. Bill reported this exchange to DS Alex Cameron and DC John Wallace at Maryhill CID. He supplied the name of the taxi driver and his brother, but neither were ever spoken to by the police. The failure to acquire the phone number being actively used by Lawson, against the backdrop of text threats, felt to Bill like a massive missed opportunity, even more so given what happened next.

The following day, 3 August, Bill was transported to the city's sheriff court, where he was released on bail into the arms of Jackie, who had had little sleep in the past two nights. The couple drove straight from court to the retail garage premises in Hyndland of friend and business associate Michael Lyden to collect a stored car. That night, some of Lyden's vehicles, parked on the street outside his garage, were vandalised. Three days later, on 6 August, both Lyden and Bill received some nasty text messages. Lyden was warned that if he did future business with Bill then his garage would be torched and his family targeted.

The text also included Lyden's home address. The message to Bill tauntingly asked, 'Did we do a good job on the 3 cars?', an apparent reference to the Bearsden incident. It ended with the chilling threat:

Next it's a blade in the ribs or a bag of smack.

Crucially, the texts were sent from the same number. That they linked the Bearsden attack to threats to burn down a garage and the use of a knife against Bill – and a threat to plant drugs – could have been evidential dynamite. Proving who sent the texts may not only have potentially helped nail who was behind the long-running vendetta, but was also pertinent to the live investigation into the Lawson stabbing. Surely the police would urgently want to know about a subsequent threat to use a knife? Did these messages back up Bill's claim that the blade belonged to Lawson and that he was the aggressor?

Lyden reported the texts at his local police station in Partick while Bill reported his to DS Cameron and DC Wallace, despite his lack of faith in them. It was DS Cameron who had previously issued Bill with an unmerited warning to behave, which fed the false narrative of a 'feud'. It was DC Wallace who had enraged Bill in Bearsden with the series of questions suggesting he was a suspect not a victim.

Inaction ensued. Just as the police did not bother speaking to the taxi driver who was in possession of Lawson's phone number, little happened. Yes, Lyden gave a statement to the police, but he heard nothing more.

The text messages only underwent cursory investigation a year later, after continued agitation by Bill. Many years after that, Bill discovered that DS Cameron and DC Wallace had come up with an interesting explanation for their initial inaction: they got confused. They thought these texts were old and therefore related to a previous crime.

The following month, CCTV cameras at Bill's home captured clear images of a mystery man in his driveway, attempting to break into a car. DC Wallace was dispatched to speak to Bill at home and left with a statement and a copy of the CCTV footage. Inexplicably, no crime report was raised for this incident. No crime report equals no crime. As far as the official record is concerned, it did not even happen.

Bill was powerless. Forces outwith his control were at play. Supposedly innocent until proven guilty, it did not feel like it. As far as some police were concerned, he was a dangerous criminal. Being charged was enough to taint his reputation.

For nearly three years the criminal vendetta had consumed Bill's life. On the plus side, after Lawson's stabbing, the crimes effectively ceased, other than a couple of minor incidents. Bill did not regard this as a coincidence.

Almost another three years would slowly pass before he would get the chance to clear his name in front of a jury of his peers. During that time, his life was suspended in purgatorial limbo, as the case became entangled in the opaque corridors of the Crown Office and, from there, limped interminably through court. He did not sit back passively.

24

IN EARLY COURSE

While Bill was in limbo awaiting trial for the stabbing of John Lawson he received a surprise invitation to meet one of the most senior CID officers in Glasgow. It was eight months after the Lawson incident and policing was being overhauled, with the country's eight regional forces replaced by the single entity of Police Scotland.

In the dying days of Strathclyde Police, Bill had written to the acting chief constable, providing him with a detailed account of the fake criminal record and the vendetta being waged against him and Jackie. A couple of weeks later, just after the nationwide force was born in April 2013, the letter resulted in Bill being asked in for a chat by Detective Chief Inspector Stevie Grant, soon to be promoted to Head of CID for Greater Glasgow and the boss of many officers Bill had experienced problems with. It was an unusual occurrence for someone charged with a serious crime of violence, and the source of multiple complaints, to have a friendly and informal face-to-face with an officer of such high rank. Grant, a plain-speaker, assured Bill there would be no 'bullshit'. Sitting in on the meeting was someone whom Grant introduced as an IT expert; this person stayed silent throughout, watching from the sidelines. Bill left with the suspicion that his true purpose had been to get the measure of him – and find out what he knew – than any new-found desire to vigorously investigate.

Bill recalls: 'Grant and this other officer led me through a maze of corridors to this little interview room. I'd been told I would not be bullshitted and hoped that would be the case but almost straight away I could see it for what it was – an intelligence-gathering exercise. They wanted to assess what type of person I was, what I knew, my understanding of their systems, whether I posed them any threat.

'I actually said to Grant that if the other guy was really an IT man then I was Donald Duck. I believe that he was there to watch me and listen to my answers. I told Grant that if he really was an IT guy, he could find out in two minutes how I had been given the criminal record. They provided no clear answers to my questions, but it was still worthwhile because it informed me how they were thinking and also allowed me to tell them what I wanted them to know.'

Good riddance Strathclyde but, alas, Police Scotland seemed no better. Other than the name, it soon felt like nothing had changed. The consequence of the meeting was for Grant to appoint Detective Inspector Stevie Watson to conduct a three-pronged investigation.

In June 2013, Watson was tasked with examining how Bill had been assigned the record, how it was allegedly leaked, and to review how each of the dozens of crimes inflicted against him had been dealt with. Watson had plenty to get his teeth into and Bill hoped for a speedy turnaround, given that so much precious time had already been squandered by squabbling. Over several days, he provided Watson with a meticulously detailed statement, running to 38 pages.

In a second letter to the police a few months after the first, Bill imparted fresh claims relating to the alleged disclosure of the bogus record to White by an officer. That led to both MSP Sandra White and fellow SNP MSP Bill Kidd being interviewed as part of Watson's enquiry, which was picked up by myself for the *Sunday Mail*. It reported:

> Two MSPs have been interviewed by detectives after a police officer was accused of leaking confidential criminal records.
>
> They are investigating claims that MSP Sandra White was wrongly told a constituent had a serious criminal record by an officer.
>
> The Glasgow Kelvin politician, 62, and fellow SNP MSP Bill Kidd, 57, who represents the city's Anniesland constituency, were interviewed as witnesses by police and asked if they were made aware of the man's alleged criminal record.
>
> The information is held on police computers and can only be used for legitimate crime-fighting purposes.
>
> Police Scotland have since admitted the convictions belonged to someone else. The constituent has no criminal record and believes his details were added to the wrong criminal record after he complained about a police investigation into a fire attack on his business premises.

I also sought a response from White, who told me: '[The police] spoke to me, asking the same questions you did. I know absolutely nothing about it. If any criminal record has been wrongly attributed to somebody, a member of the public, it should be looked at.'

Because Bill was awaiting trial for the Lawson stabbing, contempt of court laws prevented the newspaper from naming him – even though he desperately wanted his story told. Contempt laws are supposed to ensure a fair trial by banning the reporting of details of cases before they reach a jury. But the interpretation of what can or can't be reported differs greatly, depending on which lawyer you ask. In addition, many cases are ultimately never heard by a jury, while others limp through courts for years. Therefore, criminals who deliberately delay, or 'churn', their prosecutions, using time as a weapon, benefit from an effective media blackout on their nefarious activities. Some critics believe contempt laws are past their sell-by date in the digital age, as background information is often online.

Anyway, jurors are told to only consider evidence presented in court. In this case, the consequence of the unpredictable contempt culture was that it curtailed Bill's right to speak publicly about a gross injustice. Any publication or broadcaster who had defied their own legal advice to give him a platform would have risked being criminally prosecuted, with a jail sentence as possible punishment for the editor. A cynic might think that in toxic cases such as Bill's, contempt law serves as an insidious tool for the authorities to keep a lid on scandals and mouths shut.

When Bill first sat down with Watson there was an initial rapport. The officer seemed open and decent. Against his better judgement and experience, Bill felt a flicker of cautious optimism and prayed that it might just be a turning point.

By the end of 2013, those hopes were extinguished.

His first concern related to the MSPs. Bill had made an explicit allegation of criminality against a named police officer for leaking the record. According to Police Scotland's rules, this allegation should have been forwarded to the force's professional standards department (PSD). From there, if any evidence of criminality was found, it should have been reported to the Crown Office's Criminal Allegations Against the Police Division (CAAPD) in Edinburgh. Bill believed he had produced prima facie evidence that criminality had occurred. But the enquiry remained ring-fence by CID and was not passed to professional standards or the Crown – not that Bill knew any of this at the time.

As months passed, Bill formed the opinion that Police Scotland had decided to tread water – waiting for his criminal trial to conclude before producing their report. It made sense. If he ended up convicted, he could have been dismissed as just another jailed thug with an anti-police agenda. Fake criminal convictions? So what? He would by then have a real one.

By May 2014, almost a year after first sitting down with Watson, Bill emailed him his concerns about the delay and how the evidence relating to the MSPs was being dealt with.

He wrote: 'It would appear this whole situation is being suppressed and it is time your report was concluded to allow me to take the next appropriate steps, although I suspect you have no intention of concluding the report prior to my trial.'

In response, Watson offered 'a comprehensive undertaking on my part to ensure all matters are thoroughly investigated' and denied that any delays were linked to Bill's trial. He added, 'I can categorically state there is no suppression abound here and that I hope to have this complete and in the hands of my supervisor in early course.' Bill ought to have asked Watson to define 'early course'.

Between the period from 2014 and throughout the following year, Bill continued to agitate and object about the lack of progress, always doing so in writing.

One such dispatch read: 'I now have no confidence in the police whatsoever as it is now clear that their self-interest and reputation are paramount at any cost. We have had five years of damage already, so if the police are prepared to start some straight talking then I am ready to listen.'

Bill engaged Paul Langan, a criminal lawyer and friend, to increase the pressure. Langan obtained a legal opinion from Paul Nelson, the advocate who would go on to defend Bill in the stabbing trial. Nelson's view was that the police already possessed sufficient evidence to report Lawson to the Crown in order to bring a criminal prosecution.

Another unusual development took place. Some 15 months after embarking on his report, Watson asked Langan and Nelson to come and see him. The lawyers – and Bill – were surprised but pleased. According to the legal duo, Watson gave an undertaking to send a report about Lawson to the Crown. Whatever Watson's intentions may have been, it did not happen, prompting Langan to write to him in January 2015.

Langan stated: 'We are extremely surprised and disappointed to learn that the report against Lawson had not yet been submitted. We had understood that the report would be submitted to the Crown very shortly after our meeting with Mr Nelson as far back as September [2014].'

Watson, repeating the language of earlier, replied that his report would be finalised, 'in very early course', specifically 'by next midweek'. His email, dated 22 January 2015, added: 'Once this is done, again in early course, thereafter it is my intention to report the history of criminality suffered by Mr Jonhstone.'

It turned out that Watson did not produce his report the following week. It took another four months. And, just as Bill had predicted, Watson only delivered it *after* the criminal case finally ended. When it arrived, its findings did nothing to alleviate Bill's concerns, they only spawned yet more wearisome paperwork and sent him back into the maze of complaints. Furthermore, Watson never sent a report about Lawson to the Crown.

25

JUSTICE DELAYED

A famous Greek myth tells how Tantalus spends eternity standing beneath a fruit tree in a pool of water, both of which remain just out of reach. While Detective Inspector Stevie Watson's report remained stubbornly elusive for years, just as tantalising was Bill's glacially slow quest for justice after being charged with stabbing John Lawson.

He first appeared in court in August 2012, his 55th birthday. Almost three years later – in March 2015 – his trial took place. During this time, his tunnel-vision determination for answers consumed too many hours, occupied too many conversations and ate into the fabric of everyday life, which often caused Jackie to shake her head in despair. While Bill's torture did not last an eternity, those three years felt interminable.

It was only in May 2013 that the police, for the first time, explicitly admitted in writing that the criminal record did not belong to him. A civilian employee stated, 'Please be assured that the record sent to the procurator fiscal at that time was not and had never belonged to you.' This basic and grudging admission, with no explanation and a refusal to answer other key questions, came a full two years after Bill was handcuffed at the roadside as a wanted man. The fight on that particular front would rumble on for many more years.

Courts are blighted by a culture of delays, and Bill's 'churn' was unusual in that other than six weeks lost due to his lawyer having a diary clash, the entirety of the delay was down to the Crown.

There is a clear legal requirement for the police to tell the Crown what it knows. The same applies to the Crown, which must then share the information with an accused person. These rules exist to ensure the right to a fair trial. The bad old days of unhelpful evidence being buried by police and prosecutors are supposed to be over. In 2010, just months after Bill's garage fire, Strathclyde Police's then chief constable Stephen House explained what is expected: 'In any criminal proceedings in Scotland, disclosure of relevant material to the accused is a fundamental requirement of criminal justice in accordance with Article 6 of the European Convention on Human Rights. The duty of disclosure falls to the Crown; however they can only discharge this duty satisfactorily if police officers reveal to them the existence of all material which may be relevant and has been obtained in the course of investigations.'

The year after House's instruction, a new law came into force which enshrined the need for police to share with the Crown, and the Crown with defence, 'all information that may be relevant to the issue of whether the accused is innocent or guilty'. A generously broad definition is applied to what is 'relevant', it being 'information that appears to have some bearing on the offence or under investigation or any person being investigated or on the surrounding circumstances, unless it is *incapable* of having any impact on the case'. For the police and Crown, 'disclosure carried out properly and timeously ensures that justice is done and prevents unnecessary trials and delay', while suppressing inconvenient truths 'risks a miscarriage of justice'. Given all of that, it should be safe to assume that disclosure is hard-wired. In the case of *HMA v William Rodgers Johnstone*, that assumption was incorrect.

A pattern to the delays emerged. Bill and his lawyer would attend court and seek disclosure from the Crown. The Crown would not be in possession of the required information from the police, so they would request a delay from a sheriff, who would oblige. And on it went.

In August 2013, more than a year after being charged, there was a hearing in which the Crown argued that Bill's bogus record and crime vendetta was not relevant to the stabbing trial. It was an odd position, given the legal test of it needing to be 'incapable' of impacting on the case. The sheriff disagreed and ordered the Crown to disclose to Bill's lawyers the full and extensive background.

Two months later, in early October, everyone was back in court to hear there was still no sign of the information which the sheriff had ordered to be disclosed. The prosecutor vowed 'that this should be chased up as a matter of urgency, we now anticipate that they should be forthcoming in the near future'. Two weeks after that, in late October, they were back again . . . yet there was still no full disclosure, the release being slow and piecemeal. On this occasion, the Crown requested the sheriff grant an extension to the time bar, giving them longer than they were legally entitled to prepare their case. They also asked for new police officers to be added to the list of Crown witnesses. Bill had gone to court that day with the intention of opposing any fresh attempt by the authorities to buy time, but changed his mind on the basis that these new witnesses were immersed in the non-disclosed background which would allow his defence to introduce the murky topics of a fake criminal record, the involvement of two MSPs and police failures to investigate a crime vendetta.

Bill did not appreciate it immediately, but this was a pivotal period. During one of the many court hearings, a procurator fiscal told a bemused sheriff that Bill's case file was missing. In fact, he later discovered, it had been sent down the M8 for high-level consideration at the Crown's HQ in Edinburgh. Up until then, the Crown had been largely oblivious to the ugly background, because the police had withheld it, contrary to the law. Once the Crown finally prised disclosure from the police, two things could have happened. The Crown could have slammed on the brakes and ordered the police to conduct a proper investigation into the fake record and the spate of crimes suffered by Bill, the outcome of which would have presented a very different story to the one the police had told and may have even derailed Bill's prosecution entirely, if not ensured its honesty. Or they could have absorbed the police's grudging and shocking revelations and then tried to shape them to the prosecution's advantage, no matter how unwieldy, selective or unjust. That is what they chose to do.

Seasoned criminal lawyer Paul Langan sat Bill down in his office and explained that the Crown, having dragged the truth from the police, had decided to up the ante. They were *not* going after Lawson; they were certainly *not* interested in going after the police. They were going for Bill's jugular.

The Crown's decision to introduce certain police officers to the witness list indicated a fundamental change in strategy. If the criminal vendetta could no longer stay buried, then it could be used against Bill. The prosecution would argue that he had a motive to stab Lawson by portraying him as a dangerous obsessive, immersed in a vendetta and bent on revenge against his tormentor. In order to paint that picture, the Crown introduced police statements in which four officers made such claims.

They included DC John Wallace, who had attended at the three trashed cars in Bearsden on the day of the Lawson stabbing. He gave a statement saying that Bill was so angry he had threatened to take matters into his own hands. DS David Patrick provided a similar statement, in which he described Bill as 'obsessive'. As the 'reporting officer' for the stabbing, Patrick's job should have been to disclose all relevant background to the Crown.

By the time 2014 came along, a betting man would have got pretty long odds on Bill's chances of beating the rap. With the Crown and the police taking the fight to him, he responded the only way he knew how: by counter attack.

Langan wrote to procurator fiscal Celia De Groute in March 2014:

> As you are aware, the accused [Bill] contends that this [fake criminal record] was not done simply by mistake but in fact was borne out of malice. You will appreciate that there are remarks which have been attributed to the accused which will be challenged by him, and this piece of information is deeply relevant to the accused's line of defence. Indeed we would suggest that the existence of the criminal record has clouded and hampered the police investigation of the numerous crimes of damage to property and threatening text messages.

As Bill faced 'solemn' proceedings, in which a jury would decide his fate, and his freedom was on the line, he was entitled to seek legal aid to pay for senior counsel, rather than rely solely on a criminal defence solicitor. His application for senior counsel stated:

> The attributing of the accused with a criminal record is significant in that police officers who may have attributed him with the record are due to give evidence in

the case of a remark allegedly made by the accused some months before and indeed on the date of the incident which would provide corroboration for the Crown's case. It is, therefore, highly important that this information is obtained to undermine the validity of the police evidence in this case. These very same officers are under investigation following upon the accused submitting a complaint against them.

The application was successful and Bill's defence team was bolstered with the addition of advocate Paul Nelson, who quickly grasped the extremely unusual nature of the case and embraced its challenge. As a former prosecutor, he knew their tactics and tricks. While Bill's opinion of the police and Crown had never been high, it sank even further during that long ordeal of opaque legal chicanery.

Bill surmised: 'The CID fitted me up with a fake record and they kept it and everything else from the Crown for years, but when the Crown eventually found out the truth, nothing changed – the fit up became an attempted stitch up. I am not paranoid, I've seen dirty tricks in the criminal justice system, and it was blatantly obvious that they were determined to convict me of the stabbing, even if that meant playing fast and lose with the rules, not least regarding disclosure. The police chose to bury the long history of crimes involving Lawson because it was so toxic to my prosecution. When that failed, the Crown decided to use it against me by telling a jury that I was a dangerous and unreasonable person with a score to settle.

'It is disgraceful that the Crown also disregarded my detailed allegations and clear evidence of police negligence, misconduct and criminality, but if they thought I was running scared they'd be wrong. If the Crown wanted to get the CID to say I was an obsessive who had stabbed

Lawson in revenge, that suited me just fine. My freedom was at stake, but I wanted nothing more than those detectives in front of a jury and under oath.'

26

TRIAL: STAR WITNESS

On the morning of Bill's trial, minutes before he was due to stand in the dock as an accused man, his mobile rang. It was the CID with an urgent request – they wanted his fingerprints. Bill's advocate Paul Nelson listened in to the peculiar call, shook his head in wry disbelief and suggested to his client not to go anywhere near any CID officer. It was the third such call from the detective in a matter of days. The male officer, whose name was not familiar, explained that he was investigating the razor blade posted to Bill and Jackie's home and needed their prints for elimination purposes. The call came as the trial was set to begin on 9 March 2015. Yet the blade had been handed to the CID in December 2009. It was a strange take on 'urgent'.

Bill initially suspected that the CID were playing games, that badgering him may have been intended to distract and unsettle just when he was steeling himself for his long awaited chance of justice. He later revised that theory. By then, Detective Inspector Stevie Watson was almost two years into his plodding, three-strand investigation of how Bill had been given a criminal record, how it was allegedly leaked and how police had handled the many crimes he had suffered. The razor blade presented a tricky loose end.

Bill's first complaint had been about the botched investigation into the destruction of Turnberry Motors, led by Detective Constable Campbell Martin. When the blade arrived in Bill's mail the following month, the same officer requested that he take charge of that investigation too. Almost immediately, protocols were not followed. It took further complaints from Bill and his lawyer before an incident number and crime report were raised. Martin then stated that the blade would be submitted for forensic and fingerprint tests. But, almost six years later, it had not happened. It made sense that Watson would seek to get it done, even if only for the sake of completeness rather than any realistic likelihood of a breakthrough.

But why were the CID scrambling around and pestering Bill on the morning of his trial, to the extent it felt like interfering with a witness? To Bill and his lawyers, the answer lay in the fact that Martin was police witness #3 of 26 officers listed by the Crown.

Bill explained: 'All those years earlier, Martin said the razor blade crime report should be closed pending the outcome of fingerprint analysis, but this was never done and it was only when Watson was reviewing the dozens of crime reports that it was discovered. They knew that Martin and his CID colleagues were due on the stand, where they would face very difficult questions about that and the many other chronic failures. While there was no real prospect of yielding anything from the prints, it would at least allow them to say they had done the tests. It was a case of better late than never and a typically cynical example of doing the right thing for the wrong reasons. Mr Nelson advised me to steer clear of the CID. We had the more important matter of the trial to contend with.'

Bill pushed the distraction to the back of his mind and made his way into the court room, where 15 primed jurors were seated in silence, Sheriff Kenneth Mitchell glowered from the bench and prosecutor Ruth Ross-Davie organised her paperwork, ready to argue Bill's guilt.

The Crown's star witness was John Lawson, then aged 57, who shuffled into the stand while wearing a blue anorak and dark grey jumper. Describing himself as a welder, Lawson's account began with the description of having met with a female client and then phoning another one to discuss a job the following morning. His early testimony prompted a chiding from the sheriff, who said the case would proceed more swiftly if 'you listen to the questions'. That intervention did the trick, prompting Lawson to state, 'I was attacked and stabbed on the way up the hill.'

Upon hearing footsteps approaching from behind, he turned around to see Bill, who he then identified by pointing towards him in the dock.

Lawson said: 'He was about 50 feet away from me. I thought it was weird. I just stood; I couldn't fathom why he was coming towards me. He got closer to me and I can't remember details. We ended up close together, about a yard.

'He didn't say anything. I can't remember if he said anything. I gave a statement to the police and the details are in there. Yes, I think he said something. I was just standing there. I couldn't fathom out why he was there. I felt a push, it was jaggy. I thought it was a punch to my left arm.

'As I looked down I saw a blade sticking out of his hand and I thought the blade was covered by a white bag. I thought I had to get away. His hand was down at his side. I then realised he's stabbed me. I wasn't thinking about the pain. I was just thinking "I've got to get away." It just felt a bit sore. He just started stabbing me again.'

Making a thrusting gesture with his clenched hand, he continued: 'He stabbed us through the arm and in the back, behind my collar bone.'

Lawson, dripping with blood, then made his way towards a property where he had previously done work and pressed the intercom. He told the female occupant, a retired university lecturer in her seventies, that he had been stabbed, but she declined to open the outside door. Eventually, as a result of Bill's 999 call, police officers arrived.

The prosecutor ended her questioning, making way for Bill's defence.

Nelson took Lawson back to the beginning and the April 2009 dispute over the Ford Transit van. The lawyer then asked Lawson if he knew about the burned down garage, the litany of text threats and destroyed cars suffered by Bill. Lawson conceded that he did because the police 'went round all the people he [Bill] had a grievance with'. When Nelson suggested that Bill blamed Lawson for it all, he admitted, 'Yes, according to the police.'

Having elicited the back story for the jurors, Nelson concluded by putting it to Lawson that he was a liar – that he was in possession of the dagger and that he attacked Bill, after being confronted and warned to end the crime spree.

Lawson replied, 'I didn't have a knife. I don't carry a knife. I've never carried a knife.'

The second witness was the lady who answered her intercom to Lawson. Bill was surprised to see that she was allowed to give her evidence from behind a screen – invisible to the public and only seen by himself, the sheriff, jurors and opposing lawyers. This special dispensation was granted because the witness suffered from an anxiety disorder. However, this was not explained to the jurors. In the absence of any explanation, he believed they may have formed the view that the nervous witness was scared of him, that he was a dangerous individual who posed some kind of menace. Why else would she merit special treatment?

The witness told how she was in her kitchen when she heard 'loud sharp cries' coming from the lane below, but she did not go to her window because during an unrelated, previous occasion, items had been thrown at it. She twice rejected Lawson's pleas for access because 'in previous years there was an encounter when different things happened when I had young children', but she did agree to dial 999. Eventually, she went outside to find 'blood everywhere' and a uniformed police officer who instructed her to return indoors. Sheriff Mitchell thanked the witness, whose evidence did nothing to incriminate Bill. However, to Bill, the use of a protective screen still felt like a prosecution dog whistle, a touch of theatre which hinted at his guilt.

The final Crown witness on the first day of the trial was a 32-year-old community psychiatric nurse who had been sitting in Crown Terrace in her parked car, talking to a friend by phone. She recalled seeing a man with a white bag in his hand, who came and went from the area over around 30 minutes. She then saw a blonde woman and another man on a phone – not the same man as the bag carrier. It sounded like this couple were Jackie and Bill. If so, the jury may conclude that Bill was *not* the man with the white bag. Under cross examination by Nelson, the nurse said that the first man – with the bag – had also urinated against a Jaguar car. Asked specifically if the man using a phone was different to the one with the plastic bag, she firmly replied, 'Yes.' For a Crown witness, her testimony was not helpful, nor merely neutral, but *damaging* to the prosecution case, as it crucially seemed to support Bill's claim that it was Lawson who had the bag with the knife. As the court adjourned, Bill was buoyant. The next day's first witness would be Jackie. Then Ross-Davie would turn to her list of 26 police witnesses.

27

THE TRIAL: WITNESS #10

Day two of the trial led with Jackie Mills, who looked like she would rather be anywhere else, her jangled nerves exacerbated by a tone of tetchiness between the prosecutor Ruth Ross-Davie and Sheriff Kenneth Mitchell.

Jackie began by explaining how she and Bill had spent a long time playing a weary game of cat and mouse with their tormentor, trying to stop valuable cars being destroyed by parking them up side streets far from home. Jackie went on to say that John Lawson was responsible for the extensive crimes which they had suffered. She said, 'I believe it was John Lawson, because it had been ongoing for a number of years.' Asked why she thought it was him, she said: 'Because he had threatened to.'

During the questioning of Jackie, on three separate occasions Sheriff Mitchell intervened in order to correct or chastise Ross-Davie. In the final intervention, following a flurry of questions, he dryly asked her, 'That's three questions there, which would you like her to answer first?' This set the tone of the trial.

Of the night in question, Jackie explained they were driving past the Rock pub when they saw Lawson going up a side street. When Bill exited the car to pursue him on foot, she said she 'wasn't awfully happy about it'. She explained: 'Some of the cars had tyres stabbed and I was worried because I've always been of the opinion that John Lawson carries a knife.'

At times, Jackie's quiet delivery became almost inaudible, earning a prompt from the sheriff to speak up. While her words did not fill the large room, they were steady and sure, not least in respect of the white plastic bag which may have contained the knife that injured Lawson. Jackie was certain that when she first saw Lawson going up the side street, he had 'something white in his hand', believing it to be a towel or hankie, adding, 'I later found out it was a plastic bag.'

Once she arrived at the bloody crime scene, she saw Bill on the phone, with his foot on top of the bag. She said: 'I picked the bag up because a car was going to drive up the street. I didn't want them to drive over it. I put it down nearer the side where it wouldn't get run over by a car. I thought it would be evidence with fingerprints. I saw the pointed edge sticking out.'

She confirmed to defence lawyer Paul Nelson that no attempts were made to hide the bag or blade.

The initial police witness was PC Michelle Burns, as she and a male colleague had been the first to arrive in response to Bill's 999 call. Nothing in her evidence was contentious. The second was PC Roddy Shaw, who was tasked with guarding the cordoned-off crime scene. As he spoke, what he described as a 'commando dagger' in a sealed plastic tube was produced and shown to the jurors and sheriff.

The third officer called by the Crown was PC Suzanne Walker – Crown witness, #10 – who was aged 30 and who entered the stand while carrying a large Primark shopping bag before sitting down to give evidence. At this, the sheriff's eyebrows rose in puzzlement and he asked why she was not standing. From a bad start, it did not get any better. Once Walker took to her feet, she began by saying that she had been assisting the CID in August 2012 when she attended the call to Bearsden with Detective Constable John Wallace, where a Subaru, Mercedes and Audi lay wrecked. She described Bill as being 'very animated' and then delivered a claim that had the potential to send him to prison.

According to Walker, as Bill ranted about the trashed trio of motors, 'he didn't know how long until something was going to be done about it, words to that effect. He was going to take matters into his own hands.' This was the moment that Bill had been fearing; the moment the police and Crown went on the attack. Their weapon – the toxic claim that he had threatened vigilante action hours before Lawson was stabbed.

Nelson's skilled cross-examination was going to be vital. Having ascertained that Walker knew of the extensive background of crimes inflicted against Bill and his property, the defence lawyer asked about the claim she made that he intended to take matters into his own hands. She replied vaguely that it was 'something along those lines'. Nelson tried again, prompting the admission that she could not 'recall specifically word for word'. Sheriff Mitchell interrupted to ask, 'Why not write them down at the time?'

'Because DC Wallace was taking the details of it,' she replied.

Nelson then asked, 'You were there to corroborate?'

'Yes,' she replied, followed by a meek and weak explanation. 'It was two-and-a-half years ago.'

Displaying a mixture of incredulity and disdain, the sheriff interjected, 'That's precisely the point. If you'd taken a note you would be able to look at your note.'

Compounding the mildly farcical nature of Walker's evidence, she admitted that her statement was timed as being given at 9.45 p.m. when it should have been 1.45 p.m., this being explained as an 'error by the typing pool'.

During Nelson's questioning of the hapless officer, he pointed out that there had been a 'campaign of terror, 20 or so complaints to the police and apparently nothing had been done' and that Bill's exasperation was due to the 'inactivity of the police'. This was hardly Walker's fault, as her only involvement in the saga had been the day she accompanied DC Wallace to Bearsden. But the same awkward questions were primed and ready to be put to DC Wallace and the other CID officers on the Crown's witness list. Nelson would forensically question them about the astonishing and lengthy catalogue of failures, beginning with the garage fire six years earlier. More tricky still were their claims that Bill had threatened to take matters into his own hands.

Given how Walker fared on the stand, with that allegation crumbling under the merest scrutiny, a Crown rethink was urgently required. Could they risk a procession of CID officers making similar clumsy claims while also attempting to defend the indefensible failings suffered by the accused? Clearly not.

Only one more police officer was requested – witness #13 Detective Constable Laura Crossan. Her evidence simply comprised corroboration of her 17-minute taped interview of Bill, which took place at 5.34 a.m. on the morning after the stabbing. She had nothing to say about vendettas, vigilantism or reprisals. When prosecutor Ross-Davie asked her whether she recognised the voice of the 999 caller, which was played to the jury, the sheriff again had to interject, saying, 'This has been admitted; it's not competent to bring matters that are admitted.'

Of the Crown's 26 police witnesses, only four were called. Three of them spoke to the facts directly relating to the crime scene and Bill's police interview. Only Walker was used to air the accusation that Bill was so consumed with rage that he intended to take matters into his own hands.

The other officers who had provided statements to that effect, to varying degrees, were spared the ordeal of scrutiny under oath. Crown witness #7 DC John Wallace, #17 Detective Sergeant David Patrick and #18 Detective Inspector Stephen Healy were stood down. Detective Inspector Stevie Watson, who had also provided an incriminating statement, was also not required. Their evidence would not be led, could not be tested.

Following DC Crossan, the Crown was chastised again by the sheriff. This time for the failure to cite Dr Monica Wallace, who had treated Lawson at A&E, leading to half a day of court time and resources being wasted.

The sheriff noted: 'It's a shocking situation to find the Crown in. I've just finished a case with one of your colleagues where as a result of which a consultant's 85 outpatient appointments were lost. I'm very concerned at the way the Crown are approaching and dealing with medical witnesses at the moment.'

The next day, Dr Wallace was present and provided an account of Lawson's injuries.

Nelson then asked for time to speak privately to the prosecutor Ross-Davie, and the court rose.

Just six minutes later, the rival lawyers came back into the room. Bill returned to the dock, a poker face giving away nothing about what deal had been reached behind closed doors. Ross-Davie turned to the sheriff and informed him that the Crown was amending Bill's charge. A pen was duly put through the damning excerpt that he had 'previously evinced malice and ill will' towards Lawson.

It was a wise decision by the Crown and was met with a mixture of relief and regret by Bill. Relief, because the nefarious suggestion that he was intent on exacting revenge on Lawson had been abandoned. Regret, because these officers would not be asked about the claims made in their statement or held accountable for the police's many actions and inactions.

28

THE TRIAL: VERDICT

Despite the Crown Office's decision to drop the police claim that Bill was an obsessive intent on revenge, the trial was not over yet. The CID's poisonous allegation had been carefully crafted only to be unceremoniously abandoned by prosecutor Ruth Ross-Davie, but his future and freedom remained in the gift of the jury.

Bill had numerous opportunities to object to the insufferable Crown churn and in doing so may well have persuaded a sheriff that proceedings should end, due to unreasonable delay. But even though standing trial was inherently risky, he wanted his story to be heard.

There were many reasons for throwing a dice in this way, one being that it would give Bill's lawyer Paul Nelson the opportunity to unpick the CID officers' claims. When that opportunity was lost after the Crown jettisoned the CID witnesses, a trial would nonetheless also allow Bill to publicly trail the horrific background of crimes inflicted against himself and Jackie. The police's abject failures in respect of the crimes would also be played out.

In addition, Bill also wanted to place in the public arena the still unexplained occurrence around which the entire saga had been spun – the devastating attribution of his name and date of birth as an alias to a serial criminal with a record of violence and dishonesty. However, Nelson had a different view. The advocate regarded the introduction of the fake record as a tactical error, as it carried the risk of appearing to be a red herring, with the possible unintended consequence of confusing and distracting the jury from its relatively simple task, which was to decide what happened during Bill's encounter with Lawson. An extraordinary account of an innocent man being smeared by police could be viewed as so implausible that it could backfire, thereby causing the jurors to question the veracity of everything else Bill said. He duly bowed to Nelson's experience and judgement, and the jury would not get to hear a word about it, presumably to the relief of the Police Scotland high command.

There was another big reason for wanting to go to trial. To have the case kicked out due to delays would feel like cheating. He wanted a public acquittal based entirely on the evidence. Having endured almost three years of delays, at long last Bill's opportunity to explain what happened that summer's night when he came face to face with Lawson in a leafy West End lane had come.

The difference in the demeanour of the two men was pronounced. Lawson had toiled uncomfortably, his eyes darting evasively and his delivery stilted, defensive and unsure, even under the gentle handling of a sympathetic prosecutor. Then there was his casual attire, which seemed more suited to a welding job than the solemn surroundings of a court.

Bill's military DNA was apparent. Every crease was sharp, his beard trimmed, shoes polished, back ramrod straight and movements swift and decisive. If the hawkish, clipped and confident demeanour did not give away his army background, the regimental tie knotted firmly around his neck would surely have informed even the least observant of jurors. When he crossed the short distance from the dock to the witness stand, he was mindful of the plaque on the wall of his former commanding officer, 'In times of stress the professional soldier must be cool and thoughtful.' There was no chance of Bill flapping or floundering. If anything, his no-nonsense certainty could be mistaken for abrasiveness and his bullishness may have benefited from being tempered, lest it antagonise any jurors.

Bill began by explaining how he and Lawson had fallen out following the Ford Transit van sale in April 2009. 'He had sold the van, he said, in order to buy that one, and he wanted £1,900 back because he lost that on the sale of his own van. He said if he did not get £1,900 he would burn the garage down.' Bill then explained how Turnberry Motors was destroyed by fire, followed by dozens of other crimes.

Nelson then asked about PC Suzanne Walker, Crown witness #10, and her claim that he 'was going to take matters into his own hands' hours prior to Lawson's stabbing.

Bill replied, 'I never said that.'

On the night of the incident, Bill spotted and followed Lawson because he feared that another of his vehicles was about to be damaged and, to his surprise, 'when I rounded the corner he was right in front of me', Bill explained. 'He shouted, "I've done your garage and motors. If you don't get tae fuck I'll tan you an' all." As [Lawson] came forward towards me I could see a couple of inches of what looked like a knife blade protruding from the bag.'

According to Bill, Lawson then lunged towards him and he grabbed his wrist in order to divert the blade. He told the jurors, 'John Lawson is a strong man, he was determined he was holding onto that knife. At that point when we fell over the wall he let the knife go but grabbed it with his other hand. I had his neck and his arm at my side. I was just hanging on for my life because if I let go of his arm I wouldn't be here today. It was like a blur. I shouted "Police, phone the police!" I kept shouting that. I didn't know at that point anything about his injuries. I realised when he got to the doorway.'

During the hour-long testimony, Nelson posed a series of simple questions:

Did you attack John Lawson?

Did you bring the knife?

Was it a deliberate attack?

Did you take the knife from Lawson and use it against him?

Did you have the knife in your hand?

Did you run away?

To each, there came the unambiguous, one-word response: 'No.'

Bill continued: 'After he dropped it I started to kick it down towards the lane. I picked it up and put my foot on it and phoned the police. Why would I leave? There was no reason to leave. I wanted to stay there to make sure the police got there with the knife. If I had left, it would have looked like you had done something wrong. Why would you?'

Nelson made way for the prosecutor, who began by asking if Bill had been happy to sell a van which he knew would fail its MOT. Puzzled, Bill explained that buyers knowingly and commonly make such purchases, which are completely legitimate. She pressed further by asking how many times he had sold vehicles without MOTs. Still puzzled, Bill replied, 'I could do it five times in one day or once every ten years.'

Next she turned her focus to the crimes suffered by Bill and his view that Lawson was responsible. Her baseless suggestion that these may have stemmed from a 'variety of disgruntled customers' was met with derision. She asked, 'Is the very idea that there was any other suspect absurd?', to which Bill answered, 'Yes.' She twice put it to Bill that he had struck Lawson repeatedly on the body with a knife, to which he twice replied, 'That's not correct.'

Finally, she asked if he was trying to tell the 999 operator that he had hurt Lawson, to which he said, 'I wasn't trying to tell anyone I had hurt anyone.'

When Nelson re-examined Bill, he archly noted, 'I'm not sure if the fiscal [Ross-Davie] is trying to see words in that [999 call] transcript that are not there.'

The advocate then returned to the everyday occurrence of vehicles being sold without an MOT and the dozens of Bill's cars that had been trashed, before concluding, 'Let's go back to the big question. Did you attack John Lawson with a knife?'

'No,' Bill replied.

Nelson then asked who had the knife and who used it, the answer to each being: 'John Lawson.'

Bill stopped talking at 4.10 p.m. and the jury was sent home for the night in order to begin deliberations the next morning, 12 March 2015.

The new day began with the closing speech of Ross-Davie, which lasted 35 minutes. She stated that Lawson had not changed his story, while Bill 'changed from one moment to the other depending on what sounded like the best story'. She described the lack of a contemporaneous notepad entry by PC Suzanne Walker as merely 'regrettable'.

She told the jury that if they believed what Lawson had allegedly said to Bill in the lane, 'that was an invitation to leave rather than fight', adding 'in any event he didn't leave, he stayed and fought and repeatedly stabbed John Lawson'. She added, 'It was a vicious and inexcusable attack, having a motive is not a defence.' She concluded by urging them to find him guilty.

Next was Nelson, who reminded the jurors that, other than Lawson himself, no one had said that Bill brought the knife. Furthermore, even the evidence of the Crown's own independent witnesses suggested it was Lawson, *not* Bill, who had been seen with the white plastic bag containing the blade.

The Crown had to 'prove beyond reasonable doubt that it was William Johnstone who brought a knife and used it', with the legal definition of assault requiring 'evil intention' – ergo, Lawson's injuries alone did not mean there was an assault.

Nelson said: 'In this case there are two stark opposites. These two positions are diametrically opposed. One must be wrong. Let's say for a minute that William Johnstone is some form of demented, knife-wielding attacker. You might think it odd that where there are no other witnesses he phones the emergency services. If you start from the position that he was attacked by John Lawson, that makes perfect sense. He had nothing to hide. He didn't have to give evidence, but he did. John Lawson has motive to lie to you to paint himself as an innocent. To say he did not have a knife; he's lying to you.'

Nelson ended his 22-minute speech by calling for a 'true verdict, that should be acquittal'.

The last words were reserved for Sheriff Mitchell, who spent almost two hours explaining legal issues, procedures and the jury's obligations. Bill's happiness at Nelson's closing speech was offset by what he perceived to be hostility from the bench and he hoped it would not infect the jurors.

After lunch the sheriff imparted a final ten minutes of instruction, before the nine men and seven women were allowed to privately debate the evidence and reach a decision. It took them 1 hour and 34 minutes to do so. By a majority, they found the Crown's case against Bill not proven. He would have preferred a unanimous and not guilty verdict, but acquittal was all that really mattered.

'Well, William Johnstone, you're free to go,' the sheriff said. And that was that.

This was not in the script.

Police Scotland had a major problem.

29

THE ARMY: GHOST SOLDIER

Anyone accessing the Ministry of Defence's record of British Army personnel from 1985 would have been able to read that Sergeant William Johnstone of the Royal Artillery's 16th Regiment was no longer a soldier, having been demobbed that August. Official records, however, are not always what they seem.

After many years of risking his life in the Northern Irish netherworld inhabited by spooks, terrorists and a certain type of soldier, it was time for Bill to retreat and regroup. Such lengthy immersion in the Troubles, the top brass adjudged, meant that he could have been compromised, offering the real possibility of his name featuring on terror gangs' hit lists. It was time to disappear.

A senior intelligence officer sat Bill down at Rapier barracks in Kirton in Lindsey, Lincolnshire, and told him to take six weeks off. He then provided him with a new identity – William Bruce – before carefully explaining how his new life was going to be. From the moment he walked out the barracks gates, he would be Mr Bruce – a coincidental amalgam of William Wallace and Robert the Bruce – with an authentic birth certificate, driving licence and other documentation, such as bank records to prove it. A British passport, also genuine, would be provided later. He temporarily kept hold of his army ID card, but it was to be destroyed.

On paper, Bill was out of the army, but his sergeant's salary continued and it began to drop into his new bank account every month and would do so for another six years until his genuine discharge. He was sworn to secrecy – even his partner Pauline, who he shared a flat with, was oblivious of his dual existence, although she often protested about his frequent and sudden disappearances from home. Bill only confided in one other person, fellow 16th Regiment soldier and lifelong friend Joe McDermott, who was also trained in intelligence.

Bill was not unique. During this time, he knew of other military personnel serving in intelligence roles who underwent a similar murky metamorphosis. In October 1984, a few months prior to his administrative reinvention at the hands of the state, the IRA had staged its most audacious UK mainland attack, with the bombing of a Brighton hotel during the Conservative Party conference. Five people, including an MP, were killed, while Prime Minister Margaret Thatcher was fortunate to escape uninjured. The Brighton bombing heightened Thatcher's resolve to drive the IRA back across the Irish Sea, and she turned to men like Bill to carry out her wishes. Far from forging a new life on civvy street, he was going deeper undercover than before.

Following his six-week break, Bill returned to his native city of Glasgow, where he opened a garage and workshop in the peripheral town of Rutherglen. Ostensibly, it was a regular and unremarkable business, but its true purpose was to act as cover for a double life. Outwardly, he was Bill Bruce, an ordinary garage boss with oily hands, dealing with customers, fixing cars – and with no military connection. Anyone who decided to poke around would find just that. Even to this day, decades afterwards, some in the motor trade still know him by his assumed name.

Meanwhile, his real job continued. He memorised phone numbers for hotlines inside two army bases in Northern Ireland, Castledillon and Bessbrook barracks, both in County Armagh, on the border with the Republic of Ireland. It was from Bessbrook that Captain Robert Nairac had embarked on his solo foray on the night of his abduction and murder in 1977. Bill used random phone boxes dotted around Glasgow to call the numbers and speak to a Military Intelligence Liaison Officer (MILO), who would then issue orders. He did not know the identity of the MILOs on the end of the secure line, although their voices grew familiar. There was no need for pleasantries or small talk. The orders ranged from simple tasks to missions which would take Bill away from Glasgow, sometimes immediately and for days on end, much to the annoyance of Pauline, who was not entitled to an explanation.

As a ghost soldier, Bill's jobs were often in Northern Ireland or England, but sometimes closer to home, as Glasgow and the west of Scotland were not short of people who vocally backed the warring Republican and Loyalist tribes across the water. The area provided safe houses, fundraising, weapons and foot soldiers. Many from Northern Ireland were drawn to Ibrox and Parkhead, where football provided a platform for their hateful religious bigotry.

It was in a Glasgow flat that on-the-run Brighton bomber Patrick Magee was captured in June 1985, weeks before Bill was handed his new ID. The police, security services and military intelligence took a keen interest in the area and prayed that the Troubles' bloodshed would not spread to the streets of places like Bridgeton and Royston.

Some tasks were simple – such as delivering a letter or package to someone in Northern Ireland. He did not need to know what it was or even who it was for. At all times, Bill wore a Browning 9mm handgun holstered to his chest. His antennae were constantly twitching, with a fine-tuned awareness of where he was and who was around. On one occasion, he and another deep-cover soldier went to meet RUC officers who had travelled to collect a suspected IRA man, arrested while attempting to sneak onto a ferry in Liverpool. The fugitive was using a US passport in another name and steadfastly maintaining he was the man in the passport, but Bill's colleague was there to confirm his true identify, having dealt with him in Northern Ireland many years before. On the way to Liverpool, a pair of curious Merseyside traffic policeman, spotting Northern Irish registration plates on Bill's car, pulled them over. Bill and his colleague stepped out and gently eased open their jackets to reveal their concealed Brownings, briefly rendering the policemen speechless.

At a police station, the incredulous desk sergeant muttered about 'bloody James Bond stuff' as Bill tried to explain who they were and why they were carrying deadly weapons. The sergeant was given a British Army number to call, where a senior intelligence officer explained the sensitive nature of the situation. They were free to go.

30

WHITEWASH

A press photographer captured the moment when Bill pushed through the court's revolving door with Jackie smiling by his side. With his open hand raised in jubilation and early spring sunshine warming his beaming face, Bill's primary emotion was euphoric relief followed closely by dark anger. Relief because a guilty verdict would have sent him to the stinking hell of HMP Barlinnie. Anger because his imprisonment, no matter how unjust, was the outcome that some police officers had plotted, hoped for and expected.

'As far as Police Scotland were concerned, I was going to jail,' Bill commented. 'They did not expect to see me acquitted.'

*

Nine months after Lawson was stabbed, Bill had contacted myself, a journalist and author. During our first meeting, the coffees grew cold as Bill imparted a complex and compelling story encompassing the garage fire, the fake criminal record, a crime vendetta, political intrigue, dirty legal tricks and a stabbing. The astonishing saga at times felt overwhelming. Could what sounded like a fantastical conspiracy theory be entirely true? It turns out that it was – and then some. At that initial meeting Bill had withheld and simplified information to avoid disbelief through overload.

Over the subsequent years of court churn, the media was prohibited from reporting on the case due to contempt of court laws, which are supposed to ensure a fair trial but too often serve to keep a lid on important matters of public interest. Only one story had been published, in the *Sunday Mail* newspaper, which explained that the MSPs Sandra White and Bill Kidd had been interviewed by the police in relation to the suspected leak of Bill's fake record. However, its impact was muted due to legal constraints.

The article had explained: 'The constituent [Bill] can't be named for legal reasons as he is due to stand trial at Glasgow Sheriff Court after an allegedly violent confrontation with the man he blames for the attack on his garage.'

With the legal proceedings finally over, the blackout ended and Bill had plenty to say. It was a *Scottish Sun* newspaper photographer who snapped Bill and Jackie as they stepped out of court. Four days later, the paper's Sunday edition carried a two-page report written by myself under the headline 'THIS IS CRIMINAL' and a sub-heading 'Ex-soldier given a fake record by rogue cop'. It told of Bill's not proven verdict for the stabbing of John Lawson and the back story leading up to it.

Bill let rip: 'I suffered a nightmare for six years. My business was ruined, dozens of cars were destroyed and my family lived in fear of fire attacks, yet the police sat back. They rushed to charge me with a knife attack which could have jailed me and has been hanging over me for almost three years.

'When I discovered that I'd been given a fake record it suddenly became clear. The police have been forced to admit it is bogus. I firmly believe that a rogue officer maliciously added it to the computer system following my complaint about the garage fire. The consequences of this fake record were massive. It meant that every time I reported a crime, officers looked at the police computer system, which told them that I was a serious criminal who was using a false name. I only found out by chance when two motorcycle cops said there was a warrant for my arrest but realised it wasn't me when they printed a photo of the person whose record it was. I was absolutely stunned, but it explained why the police had been so hostile to me. Rather than treat me as a victim they seemed to think I was committing an insurance scam.

'Even when the police removed my name from the computer system, it was still happening because there were paper copies of the record attached to my complaints. I think that senior officers realised very early what was going on but were hoping the problem would go away with me behind bars.'

Newspaper editors like stories that fit neatly into boxes and which can be easily understood and told succinctly. Those formulaic qualities did not apply here. Not only was Bill's ordeal of a highly unusual nature, its longevity, many protagonists and various interconnected strands made it a challenge to tell.

Alongside the main run of words were two smaller, separate reports. One attempted to quantify the financial cost suffered by Bill and Jackie – an estimated £500,000. The other focused on Detective Inspector Stevie Watson and his overdue report.

By this stage, Bill's disillusionment with Police Scotland was complete; he had no faith in its then chief constable Sir Stephen House or his senior management.

'They are still investigating who was responsible for the fake criminal record,' said Bill. 'But it has already taken far too long. There needs to be independent oversight because I have absolutely no trust in the police.'

A week later, Jackie broke her silence in the same newspaper in a report about her sacking by Sandra White, and the police interview of the MSP and her fellow parliamentarian Bill Kidd. Jackie laid bare her conviction that a female officer leaked the record to White and that was the reason for her dismissal.

'I expected help and support but was sacked and I couldn't understand why,' she said. 'I went to an employment tribunal but I couldn't afford a lawyer so didn't stand a chance. It was only later that we discovered Bill had been given the fake record. What happened almost destroyed me.'

White countered these claims by saying, 'I know nothing of these allegations. Ms Mills was dismissed for gross misconduct. The decision was upheld by a tribunal.'

Even after the trial was over, DI Watson still did not appear to be in any rush. Bill had long since concluded that the officer was playing a waiting game, cynically holding out for the verdict before finalising his report, contrary to his oft-stated intention to do so 'in early course', first expressed in May 2014. Had Bill been convicted, Watson's report would have been academic and could have said just about anything, as no one would have cared, or even listened, to gripes of injustice from a discredited prison inmate.

After the trial, Bill sent Watson an email:

> It is my firm position that any 'in house' investigation
> is fundamentally flawed by definition and any vestige
> of credibility was fatally compromised by your waiting
> until after the trial as I stated previously.

It was on 8 May 2015, two months after his acquittal,

that Bill received a knock at the door from a pair of CID men, who hand-delivered a brown envelope. It had taken nearly two years, ran to just 24 pages and was written by Watson's boss, Detective Chief Inspector Andrew Edward, who upheld three and rejected 12 of the 15 heads of complaint. The flaws and omissions were numerous. One issue was the 'heads of complaint' which had been defined by the police. Cherry-picked, they were framed in the woolly language of policing failures, of trifling inconveniences and oversights caused by human error and mild negligence. Some were defined as 'Quality of Service', as if Bill had merely experienced a disappointing restaurant meal rather than years of life-changing anguish caused by alleged police corruption.

Crucially, they ignored Bill's clear and repeated allegations of criminality against officers. By law, these should have been reported to the Crown Office, but they were simply overlooked. Given that Bill had been on indictment for the Lawson stabbing, such allegations should have been investigated before Bill was put in the dock, but the Crown was kept in oblivion. This failure was compounded by the fact that some of the same officers who were the subject of serious criminal allegations had been listed as Crown witnesses (albeit never called). The police, where a culture of standard operating procedures (SOPs) dictates virtually every action, appear to have flouted protocol with anarchic abandon.

At the heart of the report, for the first time, an explanation was proffered about how Bill came to be assigned a criminal record. It claimed that a civilian 'operator' – who they did not identify – had 'in error linked you to the existing record' and this had supposedly happened in January 2011, *following* Bill being charged for breach of the peace in relation to the MSP Bill Kidd. The story did not add up.

During the protracted battle with the police to disclose all relevant background information ahead of the
Lawson stabbing trial, Bill's lawyers had been sent crime
reports which documented the majority of the offences
committed against him and Jackie. One of those included
a reference number from what was then called the
Scottish Criminal Record Office. This number, unique to
Bill, linked him to the bogus record. The crime report
was dated 2010 – apparently blowing apart the police's
story about a mystery operator applying the record in
January 2011. Three other crime reports had the SCRO
numbers redacted. But when Bill held them up to daylight at the front window of his lawyer's office, the same
number was visible beneath the blacked out boxes. These
reports were also dated 2010, again pre-dating the cor-
nerstone claim that the record had been applied the
following year.

Edward, who said Watson's 'regrettable' delays 'only
served to add to your existing frustrations' upheld the following three heads of complaints numbered 7, 8 and 11:

7: A female sergeant failed to recover the CCTV of the
paint stripper attack on a blue Mercedes at Park Circus in
May 2012. Having been repeatedly told that recordings of
the private security cameras that overlooked the vehicle
were only stored for seven days, she failed to recover it.
In her defence, she blamed others and DCI Edward concluded that 'no disciplinary action will be taken against
the sergeant'.

8: Edward found Bill's accusation that the police failed
to acknowledge the seriousness of the crimes against him
'unfounded', as 'significant enquiry was conducted' into
them. However, he conceded there were 'shortcomings in
the investigation of two of the crimes', one of which being

the Park Circus crime of complaint 7. The other related
to the threatening text messages received by Bill and a
business associate five days after the stabbing of Lawson.
These texts were critical for many reasons – they linked
the three destroyed cars in Bearsden with threats to burn
down a garage, the threatened use of a knife and to plant
drugs. The sender not only implicated involvement in
the crime vendetta but they should also have been of
keen interest to the detectives investigating the Lawson
stabbing. Bill had reported the texts to DS Cameron and
DC Wallace. Yet DC Wallace's name was omitted from
Watson's explanation. Instead, another officer stated that
he could not remember why no effort was made to trace
the phone number, while DC Cameron said he had confused the August 2012 texts with another batch from three
months earlier. Watson accepted the explanations and
also conceded that the mobile phone 'data is no longer
held'. Watson upheld part of complaint 8, specifically that
it would have been beneficial for a single senior officer to
have been appointed to oversee the vast number of crimes.
The next part of complaint 8 raised a chuckle. According
to Watson, advocate Paul Nelson's reasoned opinion that
there was already sufficient evidence to report Lawson to
the Crown was 'lacking in proof and certainty'. Edward
backed his junior officer by saying, 'I am not compelled
by Counsel's argument.' So, two police officers knew better than Nelson – a highly experienced criminal lawyer
and former Crown prosecutor. When Nelson heard about
the duo's apparently superior legal expertise, he was not
impressed.

11: As it could not be disputed that the bogus criminal
record was attached to Bill's name when he was reported
by the police to the Crown for the trumped-up pub incident with SNP MSP Bill Kidd, it was therefore upheld.

For this, Edward offered an apology, while sticking to the position that the fake record came about by 'error'. As to whether the record influenced the Crown's decision to prosecute Bill, Edwards added, then he could take that up with them.

Bill viewed the three upheld points as sops, which were designed to give any neutral observer the impression that the complaints process had been fair. For Watson and Edward to have found in Bill's favour, even in such a limited way, could be presented as evidence of diligence and sincerity. Edward said that he intended to speak to some unnamed officers 'in relation to their conduct', but there was no sense of accountability.

Not only had the heads of complaint been defined by the police, the majority of them were not upheld, often on the shakiest of grounds. One such example related to the suspected leaking of Bill's record to the MSP Sandra White and Jackie's subsequent sacking in 2010. Edward discounted this as impossible on the grounds that the criminal record was first applied to Bill in January 2011. Yet, as Bill had since learned, the police's own crime reports showed that the record was in place in 2010, perhaps even earlier.

Another instance of a rejected complaint related to the multiple failures surrounding the garage fire, categorised by Watson as complaints 1 and 2. This was dealt with by Watson in a remarkable manner. He simply refused to look at it. His justification for doing so? It had earlier been dismissed by another senior officer, who had conducted what Bill regarded as a similarly flawed review.

One of the most damning aspects of the Watson report was the abject failure to treat Bill's explicit and numerous allegations of police criminality as crimes. Bill had shouted it from the rooftops; sent letters and emails from himself and lawyers, proved detailed statements over many long hours in police stations. They were effectively ignored.

Any belief that Watson could act as an independent arbiter was further undermined with a line in his own report, revealing that he had been directly involved in Bill's case. Four years prior, in 2011, he had liaised with another senior officer over a previous review of the botched criminal investigations. What Watson's report did not contain, but which further eroded any notion of impartiality, was that he had provided a lengthy statement to the detectives who had worked hard to make Bill's stabbing charge stick. In it, Watson falsely stated that Bill had a previous conviction for breach of the peace. How could he get something so basic and so important so wrong? How could he be perceived as being able to act impartially?

As far as Bill was concerned, the report was an insulting and time-wasting exercise in waffle and whitewash in which criminal allegations were buried, inconvenient facts were dispelled and clumsy assumptions made – where it suited the police to do so.

Bill, his post-trial grin long gone, told the *Scottish Sun* newspaper, 'The criminal record was applied to me long before this report states. On the basis of the date being inaccurate, other claims in the report fall to pieces. I'm not in the least surprised that it's taken over two years to come up with a whitewash. What started off a fit-up has now become a cover-up. Someone within Police Scotland should realise it's better to stop digging and start telling the truth.'

31

TOOTHLESS WATCHDOG

Being subjected to six years inside the kaleidoscope of the police complaints process felt like a form of psychological punishment dreamt up by a particularly sadistic military captor. Just as well Bill was trained in how to withstand real torture; his police ordeal was far from over.

Lawyer Chris Rogers wrote to DCI Andrew Edward to 'categorically reject' the report produced by he and DI Stevie Watson. His letter asked Edward to explain how he had arrived at the position that the fake criminal record was first applied in January 2011 – given that it featured on crime reports dated 2010. Six weeks later, Edward replied and stuck to his original claim. He said that when an earlier crime report had been created it did not contain the SCRO number which linked to the record. It was only when the police's crime management computer system was updated that the crime report was also updated to then include the bogus criminal history.

Edward then strayed into supposition, adding, 'Whilst I cannot ascertain exactly what update caused this to occur it is likely that it was a fresh crime report being raised . . .'

He went on to provide another example to support his claim, citing a mobile phone number which he said was first used by Bill from December 2011. Therefore, just like the toxic SCRO number, it was retrospectively applied to an earlier crime report. Only one problem – the claim was incorrect. Bill had actually used that phone number since 2009 and the police knew it, as it appeared in numerous of their own documents.

Edward's initial and lengthy explanation to Bill's experienced solicitor could have been construed as patronising, with the following, 'I appreciate that to persons who do not have a knowledge of these systems this may sound somewhat confusing, however I hope this answers your questions regarding this matter.'

To Bill, the claim about the timing of the record was nonsense. He and his lawyer identified and challenged numerous other loose threads in the police's account. These were often technical and dull but they did not stack up, despite the wooden language of officialdom and Police Scotland stationery giving them an air of authority. For Bill, to do nothing could result in the police's position to become 'true' by default. But to seize on each questionable claim served to suck him deeper still into the complaints black hole. More precious time and energy was swallowed. Between May 2015 and December 2016, many letters and emails comprising many thousands of words passed to and fro between Bill and Edward. At one point, according to Bill, the exasperated officer said, 'Why don't you just drop this and move on? What are you getting out of it?'

Bill believed that he had no choice. As much as he would have loved to fulfil Edward's plea by forgetting all about it and returning to a normal life, he simply could not. It was tedious and onerous but the burning sense of injustice could not be snuffed out. If anything, it burned brighter than ever. Also, for all that the criminal vendetta has suddenly ceased following the stabbing of John Lawson, what would happen if it started up again? Could he rely on the CID?

At home, Jackie, who did not share Bill's zeal or benefit from training in the withstanding of mental torture, knew that the minutiae would intrude into their conversation every single day of life. Frankly, she shared the same desire as Edward – that he should just drop it – but understood why this could not happen.

Central to the entire case was the question of exactly *how* the record had been applied. In that respect, Bill's doggedness began to pay off.

A five-page letter from Edward in August 2015 offering a more expansive explanation is revealing. It states that the operator had 'entered your details as being an alias of an existing record holder'. The operator had not made the link between Bill and a serial criminal by accident. They did not sit at their desk one day and randomly decide that Bill and the criminal were the same person – despite having different names, dates of birth and addresses. Tying them together was not based on the whim of a confused civil servant. No, Edward's use of the word 'alias' was a breakthrough. It meant that someone, or something, would have told the operator that the squeaky clean subject William Johnstone was in fact an identity of the criminal record holder. Bill was certain that the *someone* was a police officer and the *something* was an entry on a police computer system called the Scottish Intelligence Database, known as SID. The civilian only made the connection because a SID log entry, inputted by a police officer, would have told them that Bill and the crook were one and the same person. This did not, *could not*, have happened by accident.

Edward did not offer an explanation. Conveniently for the police, the mystery employee being blamed had 'left the organisation', so there was 'no opportunity to have them account for the error'. The employee, in Bill's view, was a hapless scapegoat who was being used to shield the real culprit – almost certainly a CID officer who had devastated the lives of Bill and Jackie with a few spiteful taps on a keyboard. Even if the operator story was true, it would surely be scandalous that the integrity of police intelligence could be so dangerously altered by a minor admin mix-up due to human error. If true, what other time bombs of misinformation may be buried deep within the database? Who else is innocently going about their business oblivious to the fact that, according to a police computer, they are a dangerous and dishonest crook, or worse, perhaps a sex offender?

Any police officer can add nuggets of intelligence to the SID. As of October 2017, the details of 447,347 individuals in Scotland were recorded on the secretive system. One of those people could be you – even if you have no criminal convictions and have never been directly involved with the police. You will likely never know if your name features. While it is an important tool in the fight against crime, particularly the organised variety, the abuse of SID has been an open secret in some circles for years. On one occasion, detectives sought to justify continued surveillance on a highly effective Scottish investigative newspaper journalist by submitting fictional SID logs about him. The reporter, who was investigated and ultimately cleared of paying for information from an allegedly rogue police officer, was subjected to colourful SID logs detailing unexplained wealth, owning private hire taxis and overseas property. Every word was a lie . . . but enough to persuade the bean counters that the costly surveillance was appropriate. Given the scope for the abuse of the SID, it is little wonder that the police high command seemed reluctant to talk about it with Bill, preferring to peg the entire blame on their former 'operator'.

During this period of letter writing attrition with Edward, Bill decided to try another route: the Police Investigations and Review Commissioner. Funded with around £4 million of taxpayers' money each year, PIRC is housed in a modern glass and steel box set in a dreary Lanarkshire business park. In its short life, PIRC has suffered much criticism, the most serious of which is its lack of independence from the police. The organisation was supposed to put an end to the perverse charade of police officers being allowed to investigate complaints about themselves and to finally give the paying public a fair means of redress.

Its boss, appointed in 2014, is Kate Frame, a lawyer who was previously in charge of the Crown Office's specialist unit, which is supposed to deal with criminal allegations made against police officers.

Like other spheres of the Crown, transparency does not apply, operating in protective secrecy with no meaningful explanations ever provided for its decisions. These accountability vacuums are perfect breeding grounds for decisions being made for wrong reasons.

Early evidence of PIRC's perceived ineffectiveness involved a complaint made against senior officers by Detective Superintendent Michael Orr. Following the collapse of a gangland murder trial in 2012, Orr was subject to an investigation which resulted in him being issued with a verbal warning, but he refused to accept it. He made counter allegations against more senior colleagues about how they had treated him, which the fledgling PIRC was quick to dismiss. Orr had the ability and knowledge to refuse to accept what looked like a whitewash, pushing for a review by Northern Ireland's police ombudsman, who duly upheld four of his complaints, which had been rejected by PIRC, and criticising its 'flawed' investigation.

At the heart of Bill's PIRC case were the questions of how and when the criminal record had been imposed on him and who was responsible. Everything else stemmed from that.

He optimistically told a newspaper: 'I still don't know who applied the criminal record, as answers from the police have been very selective. I believe that when PIRC looks at the evidence they'll see some officers broke the law.'

Privately, his hopes were low, with little expectation that PIRC was inclined or even able to unpick a complex and sensitive case such as his. His pessimism was well founded, for, just like the police, the PIRC investigators preferred to focus on issues involving matters of procedure not criminal allegations, conspiracy and cover-ups.

Bill identified 15 heads of complaint. His complaint ran to 34 typed A4 pages. But PIRC, just like the police, binned four of the 15 at the outset. They included the most crucial of them – number 5 – relating to the question of the record. Bill had urged PIRC to 'dismiss the unsupportable and preposterous position taken by the police, as it is a clear attempt to withhold the truth'.

PIRC adjudged that the police had already dealt with this point and they would 'not deal with concerns regarding the accuracy of the information provided to you'. So, no matter what tall tale the police had come up with, PIRC were not willing to revise it.

In response to the handwashing exercise, Bill wrote to PIRC: 'My entire case hinges around how I came to be falsely assigned a serious criminal record. Yet PIRC has stated that I never raised this as a formal complaint with Police Scotland. PIRC have concluded that this was merely raised by me as a "query". This conclusion is factually inaccurate. It was raised formally by me as a complaint on numerous occasions, from 2011 and onwards.'

Of the other three rejected heads of complaint, PIRC stated that the police had already answered two of them, which related to the inadequate investigation of certain crimes – even though Bill vehemently disagreed with the police's interpretation. Yes, the police had addressed *some* aspects of these complaints, but had simply chosen to ignore others, where they were apparently too inconvenient. PIRC, disinterested, swatted them aside.

The other rejected complaint – number 9 – was also about investigatory shortcomings, specifically the failure of police to trace and speak to named and willing witnesses. The reason given by PIRC was that it had apparently never been formally raised with the police. In response, Bill seethed back, 'This is factually inaccurate. I complained repeatedly and persistently to the police, often in writing through my solicitor, about these failings.'

An effective police watchdog ought to have taken Bill's complaint and conducted a proper investigation. His densely and detailed 34-page submission was not a light read. But an important complaint, featuring significant matters of public interest, should not surely hinge on whether it is easily understood.

Instead of being a truly independent entity which would force the police to answer the unanswered and investigate honestly and thoroughly, PIRC only added to Bill's frustrations and ever-growing collection of lever arch files stuffed with paperwork. Engaging with PIRC added another numbing layer of complex administration to the process. Rather than offering resolution, the former police officers and lawyers in their business park glass box exacerbated and prolonged the complaints process by drawing Bill into a battle on another front. When PIRC decided what did and did not qualify for its attention, there was nothing anyone could do about it. Bill may as well have been talking to himself. For he, and Jackie, the torture continued.

32

WITCH-HUNT

When the SNP government decided to amalgamate the country's eight forces to become the colossus that is Police Scotland, dissenting voices about the politicisation of policing, centralisation of powers and lack of accountability were drowned out by the seductive siren call that large sums of taxpayers' money would be saved. What nobody predicted was the advent of a twenty-first century witch-hunt.

Its exact genesis is impossible to pinpoint, but early signs can be found in media reports two years before the national force was born, in which a police chief issued ominous warnings about the spectre of organised crime gangs grooming and corrupting officers. Neil Richardson told how 27 such gangs were 'actively intending to infiltrate' Strathclyde Police and that it was happening on an 'industrial scale'. Threats, sex, honey traps, bribes and drugs were used to 'turn' police officers, forcing them to leak sensitive information. It was like an episode of the gnarly Glaswegian detective TV show *Taggart*, guest scripted by LA crime noir author James Ellroy.

There was at least one case matching Richardson's description. Lothian & Borders officer PC Derek McLeod stole a treasure trove of top secret intelligence about gangster Kevin 'Gerbil' Carroll, an associate of the Daniel crime gang, and sold it to the mob's drug-dealing rivals, the Lyons. When Carroll was shot dead outside a suburban Glasgow supermarket in 2010, detectives found McLeod's handwritten intelligence about him during a raid on the home of Lyons' hitman, Billy 'Buff' Paterson, who was later jailed for 22 years. McLeod, who also had a cannabis farm in his own home, was also imprisoned.

When Police Scotland emerged in 2013, a secretive unit to hunt down Richardson's imagined band of bent officers had been created. The Counter Corruption Unit was a fast track to promotion for its members, but the tactics used by some were extreme, often illegal. They operated as if it were the 1970s – throwing suspects against walls, threatening to remove children from mothers, perverting justice by wilfully disregarding glaring truths in order to make a case stick – all with the full blessing and protection of the top brass.

CCU targets were rarely criminals like PC McLeod, who in reality were thankfully rare, but rather ordinary officers who had allegedly committed data protection 'offences'. While some rogues were snared for data breaches, far too many of the rest were innocent. The charges were often trumped up. Look at any officer's 'digital footprint' and you will likely find something, anything, that could be presented as wrongdoing, one reason being the ambiguous definition of what merits a legitimate 'policing purpose' when using computer databases. In some instances, the CCU aggressively and vindictively went for police officers only after they had complained about their treatment. Data crimes were 'low hanging fruit' which served the purpose of swelling the statistics (and meeting targets), generating 'proof' that Richardson's ominous warnings of gangsters in blue were correct. But it was a self-fulfilling illusion. Between 2013 and 2017, 118 police officers were reported to the Crown Office for alleged data crimes. Just two of them were found guilty, a conviction rate of 1.7 per cent. More than half – 64 – were targeted in the first year.

An experienced detective, quoted in the *Herald* newspaper, criticised his own CCU mistreatment, saying, 'We lived in a stats-driven, bean-counting culture – working to create figures all the time. It created a warped environment, as the CCU tried to justify their existence.'

Another said, 'If they couldn't get you on something, they made sure they got you on a breach of the Data Protection Act.'

The CCU attack dogs instilled a fear of paranoia within the ranks of decent and hard-working cops. For every PC McLeod, there were scores of ordinary officers who were taught a terrifying lesson in being fitted up by their colleagues. Personal lives were ruined, careers trashed, good health turned bad. Faith in the police and in justice were destroyed. Communities suffered, as countless thousands of valuable police hours were wasted on the CCU witch-hunt and its subsequent fallout, which saw victims tied up in legal knots for years. Many of these victims had faith that good would prevail, that the CCU would be held to account. These were mostly men and women of integrity with a strong belief in right and wrong, their lives and work devoted to a criminal justice system that was now being used to crush them. Like Bill, they learned a harsh lesson in the reality of trying to complain about the police.

If Police Scotland could do this to their own, what hope for the rest of us?

The CCU was eventually shut down in ignominy – although some suspect the 'closure' was merely a rebranding. The final straw appears to have been when it illegally targeted the phones of serving and former officers to try and unmask the source of a *Sunday Mail* newspaper report which was of great public interest but had embarrassed the police. The story was about the badly botched investigation into the 2005 murder of prostitute Emma Caldwell, which is still unsolved. Of the ensuing row, Emma's family expressed 'betrayal' by the police, saying, 'Sadly, the CCU always appeared more interested in chasing journalists and law-abiding officers than those who let Emma's killer escape justice.'

While the CCU's reprehensible conduct is a dark stain on the proud history of Scottish policing, one fundamental element is often overlooked – the Crown Office, the state's prosecuting authority behemoth, which has 536 solicitors on its payroll. Crown prosecutors and detectives often have intimate relationships as they work together to bring criminals to justice but no one would dispute that it is the police who are the junior partners. Around the time of Police Scotland's birth in 2013, and with no public announcement, the Crown had launched its own specialist unit, the Criminal Allegations Against the Police Division (CAAPD). Its ten staff would deal specifically with prosecuting officers – freshly snared and delivered to them by the CCU.

A police officer who became a CCU target later used Freedom of Information law to dig into the Crown's secretive unit, with interesting results. In the period of just over three years from its inception, 353 police officers were reported to CAAPD. Of those, 113 were prosecuted, which resulted in 53 being found guilty of various, unspecified, offences – a conviction rate of around 17 per cent. CAAPD's modest success, when measured against a conviction rate of around 50 per cent for all other crimes in society, further serves to fuel the witch-hunt perception.

*

The next significant step in Bill's apparently endless odyssey came in 2016, when parts of his complaint, which were being examined by PIRC were sent to the CAAPD for consideration. Head of PIRC Kate Frame was previously head of CAAPD. In incestuous civic Scotland, a cloying chumminess can exist between civil servants, professional quango-crats and public board members, often even more so within tight police circles. Frame's past did not sit comfortably with Bill or others, who saw PIRC as a waste of time, a toothless watchdog which was much too close to the police. PIRC had only added to the confusion and complexity of his situation, spawning more letters and emails, and Frame's background at CAAPD, with its tight working relationship with the police, was at odds with PIRC's self-proclaimed 'independence'.

PIRC told Bill in early 2016 that the police had admitted that they had failed to refer his criminal allegations to the Crown, so they had now done so. Bill had made many criminal allegations, but PIRC focused only on two – the assigning of the bogus criminal record and its subsequent alleged leaking to others. A few weeks later, Frame's successor as the head of CAAPD, a lawyer called Les Brown, asked for more information from Bill, which was duly supplied in two pages of succinct bullet points. Things went quiet and weeks turned into months. Were the fine legal minds of the Crown digesting the complex complaint and conducting meaningful enquiries into it? Was Brown directing difficult questions at senior police officers? Or was Bill's file gathering dust in a lawyer's in-tray?

He suspected the Crown were not being proactive and that the scale and complexity of his case was a turn-off from the outset. He had no way of knowing but, with the help of his solicitor Chris Rogers, continued to push for answers and to cajole the Crown to look at his broader allegations of criminality, beyond the narrow confines of the criminal record and its leaking.

He unearthed official complaints guidelines which
stated that any allegation of criminality made to Police
Scotland, against its own officers, would be reported to
the Crown's CAAPD. This had not happened in his case,
just as it had not happened in the case of officers who had
made criminal allegations against the CCU. The guidelines went on to make the startling revelation, 'If you do
not have confidence reporting this to the police, you can
contact CAADP, who will ask for a report by the police.'
So, anyone too scared or disillusioned by their dealings
with the police could bypass them by going straight to
the Crown . . . only for the Crown to defer to the police
for answers. The flaws in the system were glaring. When
Bill was told that the Crown had spoken with DCI Andrew
Edward about his case, any lingering hopes he had were
virtually snuffed out.

In April 2017, 15 months after the file first landed on
his desk, Brown wrote to inform Bill that 'after careful
consideration' he decreed there was 'insufficient evidence' to take proceedings against any officer. What kept
a tiny flicker of hope alive was the caveat that Brown's
decision was taken 'on the basis of evidence presently
available'. This line may have been little more than prose-
cutorial fudge, to allude to the case not being completely
dead, but Bill grasped at it in the hope that there was still
a chance of justice, even just a scintilla.

More paperwork was generated. Bill had no option
but to formally lodge his disagreement with the Crown's
decision, which, like all such decisions, are never subject
to explanation. Default secrecy prevails in Scotland – long
after a more open prosecuting process evolved in England
and Wales.

There is no doubt that the scope of Bill's allegations
was broad, complex, unusual and serious, encompassing the malicious application of a criminal record on a

respectable former soldier; multiple botched CID investigations, some of which were tainted by the record; the fake record being leaked illegally; systemic lying and covering up; perverting the course of justice, including the withholding of evidence and a crude bid to send him to prison by fitting him up for a stabbing. The conspiratorial morass touched many police officers of varying rank.

It may all have seemed too much of a headache for CAAPD, which could instead continue to graze in the safe and familiar territory of data protection breaches by police officers.

33

NO MORE TEARS

By the time Liz Quinn lost her battle with cancer at the beginning of 2017, she had not spoken a word to her eldest daughter Jackie for nearly seven years and her middle daughter Elizabeth for almost as long. Her final bitter and angry exchange with Jackie had happened in the office of MSP Sandra White and ended when Liz told her daughter that Bill was a gangster who should be dumped.

White, a close friend of Liz, and of course Jackie's former boss, joined a large number of SNP members at the funeral, including Bill Kidd and the city's lady provost, paying respect to a fellow political traveller who had pursued a passionate and lifelong quest for Scotland to separate from the UK. Jackie did not attend, nor did Elizabeth, who stayed at home in California. When news reached Jackie of her mother's passing at the age of 78, no tears were shed. They had run dry long ago.

Many families suffer such tragic splits. Friction turns into flashpoints, which then breed factions and chasms. A stubborn silence, painfully raw and distressing at the outset, becomes entrenched. Eventually, after the initial ache of empty chairs at Christmas and the hurt of ignored birthdays, the passage of time renders the situation normal, or at least comes a weary acceptance of it. Neither side can forgive. Love cannot overcome pride. One day it becomes clear to all that there is no way back. In death, the damage becomes permanent and any regret is forever.

The catalyst for Jackie's familial destruction was the trenchant view of Liz that Bill was a criminal. But more important was exactly how Liz had come to hold those views. Jackie believes that her mum's devastating mis-information stemmed from the police, but by the time the criminal claim was proved to be baseless, the carnage had been wreaked.

Jackie, her matter-of-fact analysis drained of the high emotion which had defined the early years of estrange-ment, said, 'My mum chose to put her relationship with the SNP over me. She would have done anything to see Scottish independence and no scandal was going to get in the way of that. When I heard she had died, I didn't feel anything, to be honest. I wasn't upset. I was just cold about the whole thing because I had been so badly betrayed by her. We had always got on so well and my two sisters used to joke that I was her favourite.'

Most of Bill's energy had been devoted to trying to establish how his name and date of birth had been added as an alias of a serial criminal.

But almost as important was the question of how his fake record had become known to police officers, how that had influenced them during the criminal vendetta and whether it had reached the ears of others outwith the police.

Two stories had appeared in newspapers about how the police, entirely as a result of Bill's pressure, had been forced to interview White and her fellow nationalist MSP Bill Kidd about what they knew. The interviews were con-ducted as part of DI Stevie Watson's long-running enquiry, which was so riddled with flaws and omissions that it had become the subject of yet more complaints from Bill.

White denied being told by any police officer that Bill had a criminal record. Her colleague Kidd, however, was more expansive. In September 2013, a chance encounter between the two Bills took place. They had crossed paths last in Coopers bar in November 2010 and that meeting had resulted, months later, in trumped-up charges against Bill of making threats towards the politician. Their second chance meeting, three years after the first, was also in a traditional pub, The Doublet, which is a few minutes' walk from Coopers. On this occasion, they spoke in the Gents toilet and were alone.

According to Bill's account of the toilet encounter, Kidd said that he knew about his criminal record and it was White who had told him about it. However, two months later, in November 2013, when I questioned Kidd about Bill's recollection while researching my first newspaper story relating to Bill, he offered a different take.

The MSP told me: 'He [Bill] followed me into a toilet in The Doublet and he said basically that he knows that Sandra had a belief that he was a criminal and that he was somebody who was bad news sort of thing.'

He added: 'I said "Sandra doesn't like you" and I said, as it happens, Sandra had previously told me that she'd bought a car from him which was a dud.'

When I put it to Kidd that he had explicitly told Bill that Sandra told him about the record, he said 'No.'

The following week Jackie decided to pay a visit to a public surgery being held by Kidd, her former political ally and friend, to whom she had been election agent. During the civil discussion, lasting more than 40 minutes, Kidd still denied telling Bill that he knew he had a record. But he was more chatty with his former friend than he had been with me, telling Jackie: 'My recollection is that he said "Sandra thinks I'm a gangster or a crook" or something like that, and I said "Yes, she does" because she's said that, but just in terms of you know, "I don't like him, he's a crook or something."'

The reason for Sandra's dislike, he maintained, was because of a car which she had bought from him. He said: 'Sandra has told me, and she told me more than once, it mainly appears to be about a car or something like that and she says "He's a crook, that guy" and that sort of thing. I'm going "Aye okay" and that was it. You know what Sandra's like. Sandra said she wasn't happy because the car wasn't blah blah blah . . .'

The politician went on to say that during his police interview, which took almost three hours, he told the detectives that it was a 'disgrace' that Bill had been given the record.

Four months later, in March 2014, Jackie felt like another chat with Kidd would be beneficial so she paid a second visit to one of his surgeries. By now, Bill was trapped in court churn, fighting for disclosure from the police and Crown Office, and still another year away from standing trial and being acquitted for the John Lawson stabbing.

Talking to Jackie for the second time, Kidd returned to the subject of what he had told Bill in The Doublet. He told Jackie: 'I can't remember exactly. He said "Sandra doesn't like me, she thinks I'm some kind of big gangster" or something like that. What I remember was something about [the] police, and Sandra having spoken to the police, and I said, "I know." If I'd said anything about a criminal record, I don't know that, so I shouldn't have said "I know" because I don't know.'

Jackie then returned to the crux of the issue with the subtleness of which a skilled political interviewer would be proud. Bill, she said, was categorical about what Kidd said in the pub toilet that night, which was that Kidd had been told by White that Bill had a record.

To this, Kidd replied: 'If I said that, then I apologise, because I shouldn't have said that because I don't know that.'

With the same courtesy as before, he empathised with their ordeal and described the assignation of the record as 'bloody outrageous'.

The meeting, which had taken around half an hour, was over . . . although the subject was not. Bill felt that Kidd's recollections provided the police with evidence that White had branded him a criminal, which supported his contention of a police leak.

Yes, he had sold White an Alfa Romeo for £2,000, but at her insistence, due mainly to the fact the registration contained her initials and year of birth. But selling a willing buyer an old banger doesn't make you a criminal, gangster or crook. So where had this language come from? The police did not share Bill's enthusiastic interpretation of Kidd's words and neatly dismissed the theory that a police officer had leaked the record to White, resulting in Jackie's sacking in November 2010. The reason this was impossible, DI Andrew Edward had already explained, was that the 'operator' had first applied the record in January 2011.

By now, of course, Bill had vehemently countered this explanation by providing evidence to the police, contained in their own crime reports, that the record had been applied in 2010.

Only by providing an honest and detailed answer would the truth be known.

34

THE ARMY:
EQUALITY OF ARMS

'My dad's got a gun. It was a pistol and I saw it the other day,' the 12-year-old boy proudly exclaimed. The innocent boast, made in the austere surroundings of a baptist church hall in Glasgow, temporarily silenced the two chatting mums enjoying a catch-up over a cup of tea.

The boy was Bill's son, William Jr. His mother, who Bill had separated from years earlier, was talking to another mum, who just happened to be a police officer. William had only chimed in because she had mentioned something to do with police firearms. The youngster's well-intentioned contribution to the maternal discourse was to have serious repercussions.

A few weeks earlier, Bill had removed his leather jacket at home, momentarily forgetful of the Browning 9mm holstered to his torso. Out of the corner of his eye, he saw his son had noticed the gun. The boy said nothing. Bill could have had a quiet word, to offer some kind of explanation, and perhaps gently suggest that lips should remain sealed. However, that risked drawing further attention to it or invoking tricky questions, so he made the decision that saying nothing was the best option. Unfortunately for

Bill, his son was quite sure of what he had glimpsed and it could not be unseen – remaining lodged in his memory until the opportunity arose to offer it up as a conversation starter – or stopper, as the case may be.

The female police officer, consistent with that maxim that there's no such thing as off-duty, had heard enough about Bill's unorthodox lifestyle and military service to report the boy's comment to her commanding officer. A police operation swung into action. A judge signed a search warrant for the Cambuslang home of Bill and his partner Pauline. A police firearms team was briefed and mobilised.

Less than 24 hours after William Jr's church hall utterance, the police moved in. As Pauline prepared breakfast, Bill nipped out to fetch paperwork from his car but was brought to a halt by a shouted order to stop and put his hands in the air. With a small arsenal of firearms trained on Bill, a CID man inched forward and told him to place his hands on the car roof.

'Do you have a fircarm?' the detective asked.

'Yes' was the only response.

Handcuffs were secured around Bill's wrists and a latex-gloved hand carefully relieved him of the British Army-issue Browning.

But there was a big problem. Bill had another firearm, and this one was not authorised by the authorities. While it has long been common for soldiers to keep 'trophy' weapons from active service, the practice is not approved of by the Ministry of Defence. Bill had such a weapon – a Franchi SPAS-12 combat shotgun – which made the Browning look like a toy in comparison.

Pauline was just serving breakfast when Bill was led back inside, surrounded by a phalanx of stern-faced and armed police officers. Knowing that the search would yield the illicit firearm and ammunition, Bill directed them to its hiding place. Police sniffer dogs were brought inside and the house buzzed with activity while a similar search took place in the garage. As Bill was taken back outside, Pauline offered to keep his bacon and eggs warm . . . but he would not be back for quite some time.

He was taken to the police station in Rutherglen's King Street for questioning. Had the police simply phoned the army personnel department to check Bill's credentials, they would have been told that he had been discharged two years earlier, in 1985. Allowed to carry an army fire-arm, he claims? Absolutely not, they would further reply. As had happened with the Liverpool traffic officers, Bill needed to provide them with a direct line for Captain Michael Baker (whose name is changed here for security reasons), one of the few senior officers who knew about his status as a ghost soldier. There was a delay, as Captain Baker was in Germany on duty and not on the end of the designated line. This being the era prior to the digital revolution, with no mobile phones and emails, the police put Bill in a cell until his claims could be checked out.

After being locked up for the weekend, he was taken to Glasgow Sheriff Court on Monday morning, where a judge ordered that he should be remanded to the city's HMP Barlinnie. Once he had been processed by the prison authorities, he was told that two visitors were waiting. Captain Baker, accompanied by a detective from the army's Special Investigation Branch, was not radiating happiness when Bill was brought into a shabby interview room inside the grim Victorian-era building. Bill was told that he would need to go through the criminal justice system. While strings can always be pulled behind the scenes, knowledge of the shotgun was too widespread to be easily covered up.

At Bill's next court appearance, he pled guilty to posses-sion of the weapon and ammo. He was prosecuted in the

name William Johnstone. Not a word was said about the
Browning. Captain Baker then offered mitigation on Bill's
behalf, telling the sheriff about his long and exemplary
service to his country and also mentioned the culture of
'trophy weapons'. The sheriff then turned to sentencing.

Rather than sending Bill to prison, as might be
expected, given the seriousness of the charge, he instead
issued him with a £2,000 fine and he was free to go. Had
a gangster, even an ordinary member of the public, been
caught with such a weapon, a lengthy spell behind bars
would be almost inevitable. While Scotland's judiciary
prides itself on its independence from outside influence,
Bill believes that the sheriff's leniency may well have
been due to subtle back channel pressure being applied.
Helpfully to all involved, not a word of the case reached
the newspapers and the military authorities took no additional action against Bill.

That night over a few drinks Bill tried to explain himself
to his captain, saying that if a hit squad came crashing into
his home, he would not be 'fucking about with a Browning'.
He wanted a weapon capable of dealing with more than one
person coming through a door. He referred to the legal
phrase 'equality of arms', meaning that opposing sides are
entitled to an equivalent level of representation. The
stashed shotgun was Bill's literal version of equality of
arms. He now accepts that this self-justification did not
excuse the illegality, but it made sense at the time.

For all that this curious case had gone unreported to
the general public, it was necessary to assume that it may
have reached the wrong ears in Northern Ireland. Captain
Baker decided that Bill ought to stay away from Northern
Ireland's hinterlands for the foreseeable future, although
just a few weeks later he was needed back on the ground
there and the concerns about being compromised slowly
dissolved.

Bill's eventual retirement from the army, after 16 proud years, came in February 1991. This time it was official and he segued cautiously into civilian life, trying to become 'normal' and going on to build Turnberry Motors in Glasgow's West End.

As for his conviction, why did it not show up during his later dealings with the police? That is due to the Rehabilitation of Offenders Act which, with some exceptions, allows past convictions to be considered 'spent', helping reformed offenders to move on, and therefore it would not appear on a standard criminal record search. Only prison sentences of more than 30 months are never spent, while fines, such as Bill's, drop off after five years.

For all that Bill's shotgun conviction was not immediately visible to the authorities, it had not completely disappeared. During his many dealings with numerous high-ranked officers, they would have sight of the conviction and its existence helps to illustrate that even in the era of digital records, of computers being unable to lie unlike paper records, where documents could be disappeared, sometimes the official record is not always what it seems.

35

MONEY TALKS

Scotland's police complaints system is more bamboozling than a maze, less forgiving than quicksand. Bill viewed it as rigged, a charade which protects the guilty even when it comes at the cost of eroding public trust in the institution itself. In a mature democracy, where there are expectations of honesty, transparency and accountability from those who wield power over our lives it is not always so: protection of the police is entirely manmade. From his first complaint over the botched garage fire investigation in 2009, Bill had spent years being dangled interminably, at the mercy of senior officers, whose primary weapons have been to ignore the most pertinent points and time with which to break all but the most determined of complainers. The ethos seemed to be that the force's reputation should be protected, no matter the cost.

Friends, relatives and car trade associates, incredulous recipients of running updates (whether they wanted them or not), would ask Bill why he didn't just sue the police. Well, here's why . . . Yes, the police could distort and repel complaints ad infinitum, but any notion that the civil courts would offer a clean, affordable, swift and painless remedy to injustice would be fanciful, bordering on naive.

That is not to diminish the gratitude and respect that Bill holds for the lawyers who had been at his side through the police complaints process and the criminal trials involving MSP Bill Kidd and John Lawson. Chris Rogers had been his solicitor for more than 30 years but was also a solid and trusted friend who had never charged anything like the full rate for all the phone calls made and letters written on his behalf. Criminal defence solicitor Paul Langan had dealt skilfully with the trumped-up Kidd case. During the Lawson stabbing trial, advocate Paul Nelson's tactical decision to not confuse the jury with the incredible story about a fake criminal record had been vindicated with Bill's acquittal. Each of these three lawyers had warned Bill to varying degrees that the police were not playing fair. Upon reviewing the statements of the many police officers who alleged that Bill was an obsessive who had expressed vigilante intent towards Lawson, Nelson had dryly concluded that 'someone here is not playing with a straight bat'.

No matter how friendly or sympathetic the lawyer, they do not work for free, and Bill had parted with tens of thousands of pounds in fees, adding to the hundreds of thousands which the criminal vendetta had cost in lost business and destroyed vehicles. Money is one thing; precious and irreplaceable time is quite another. After the loss of all that time and money, he had stayed out of prison, but he had still not received any sensible answers.

Bill was under no illusion about the reality of suing. It would be no magic bullet, but he recognised that a writ arriving at Police Scotland HQ would perhaps have greater impact than an entire mailbag full of complaints. After all, money talks. By 2016, it had reached the stage where it was the only meaningful option left.

While high street solicitors deal with less serious criminal cases and everyday topics such as family law, conveyancing and employment disputes, if you want to bring a complex damages claim against the police or another public body, you will most likely turn towards those lawyers with membership of the Faculty of Advocates in Edinburgh.

The ancient institution was formed in 1532 and used to enjoy monopoly rights of audience in Scotland's highest courts – the High Court (criminal) and the Court of Session (civil). Like any monopoly, it was as lucrative to its members as it was costly and unfair to those who had no other choice but to use it. It took 458 years before the privileged stranglehold was broken, with the creation of specialist solicitors called solicitor advocates, non-Faculty members allowed to practice in the upper courts. However, the biggest beasts in Scotland's legal jungle are still members of the Faculty and if they agree on one thing, other than sniffiness towards interloping solicitor advocates, it is the need to maintain healthy fees.

Bill sought advice about who was best qualified to take his highly unusual case and was directed towards Neil Beardmore, an experienced Faculty advocate whose broad CV features varied civil cases and criminal work, for both prosecution and defence. The pair hit it off immediately, their personal connection helped by Beardmore being a former Gordon Highlanders officer who had also served in Northern Ireland and who had knowledge and respect for the type of hair-raising intelligence work Bill had engaged in.

Numerous meetings took place where Bill imparted to Beardmore his encyclopedic knowledge of events, stemming from the destruction of Turnberry Motors on a winter's night. Each time, a bill for hundreds of pounds would follow. The advocate readily grasped the essence of the case and agreed that the police had deployed 'smoke and mirrors' in their dealings with Bill. The police cover-up had evolved to become 'aggressive deception' and an attempt to 'change the narrative'.

By the spring of 2016, an initial version of the writ was lodged at Glasgow Sheriff Court. Running to 1,600 words – about the length of this chapter – it sought £150,000 from Police Scotland, although that figure was only notional and would likely rise once the full extent of the damages was assessed. The writ detailed the key events stemming from the garage fire. It stated:

> The fire investigation in 2009 was perfunctory. There was no proper investigation of the razor blade threat. The repeated property damage to the cars barely registered any police interest.
>
> The police officers involved described the pursuer [Bill] and John Lawson as being in a 'feud' and that the pursuer was 'obsessed'. Nonetheless, the police have had multiple opportunities to properly investigate. They failed to do so.

It also accused the police of failing in their duties, acting in 'bad faith' and that the criminal record was 'false and malicious'. It contested that Bill suffered 'loss, injury and damage as a result of the fault of the said police officers. The pursuer [Bill] sustained pain, suffering and inconvenience. He was defamed and slandered. He was put in fear of his life and property. His property, cars and garage were damaged and destroyed. He was prosecuted. He incurred legal costs. He sustained significant loss of earnings as a consequence of the closure of his business.'

It also addressed Jackie's woes, stating:

> [Jackie] worked for Sandra White MSP as office manager. DC Bernadette Walls from Maryhill police office was contacted in early 2010. Unknown police officers thereafter made Sandra White's office aware of the pursuer's 'criminal background'; that they should

disassociate from him; that the pursuer might be behind the fire and damage (as an insurance scam); that he was a gangster. This information could only have originated from the police.

It was after the Volvo car Jackie used was set on fire and it was evident that both Jackie and Bill were being followed that Sandra White, who had been helping up to that point, contacted Bernadette Walls at Maryhill to talk about her office security. On 20 August 2010, Jacqueline Mills was sacked.

Central to the case was the police's failure to investigate the criminal vendetta suffered by Bill and Jackie. His lawyers intended to argue that these failings breached Article 3 of the Human Rights Act – the right not to be subjected to inhuman or degrading treatment. The writ said that the 'prolonged campaign against the pursuer, [was] sufficiently serious to be classified as ill treatment and dehumanising'.

Bill was advised that the abundance of evidence meant that proving negligence was relatively straightforward, although he remained determined to make the case about willful neglect and perverting the course of justice – an altogether much more difficult prospect. That argument would be for later.

While proving negligence was the easier route, it was still far from simple. Over many years, the UK courts have consistently made it clear that the police cannot be sued for negligence. This legal shield stemmed from a series of blunders by detectives hunting for serial killer Peter Sutcliffe, the Yorkshire Ripper. A 1998 ruling stated that the police could not be held liable because of the greater public interest in protecting them from such claims.

That position was underlined in a 2015 Supreme Court ruling in the case of Joanna Michael, who was stabbed to death by her boyfriend in Cardiff in 2009. The police failed to respond to her two 999 calls before she was murdered.

Like virtually any civil claim, it would be a gamble, no matter how compelling its merits or conviction of its pursuer. Bill and Jackie grimaced when they were told how much it would cost. To prepare the case to reach the stage where it would be ready to be heard would be around £30,000. From that starting point, the costs would spiral ever upwards. They were up against a public body with infinite resources. Just as the police complaints process uses delays to sap the strength of complainers, their financial might could be used to drag out legal proceedings, slowly draining opponents' funds and killing a claim stone dead. If they lost, they would likely end up paying the police's legal fees, which would almost certainly bankrupt them. It was a David versus Goliath exercise, not for the faint of heart. Bill and Jackie decided to sell a property, a bricks and mortar retirement nest egg, in order to proceed, such was the determination for justice.

Bill recalled: 'It was never about the money, it was about putting everything in front of a judge so that they could see what had been going on. I refused to let these police officers get away with it.'

Beardmore, meanwhile, had his eyes on another claim against the police which was being played out at the Supreme Court in London. That case, brought by victims of serial rapist John Worboys, could potentially result in a profound change to the long-standing protection the police had against claims of negligence.

36

POLICING IN CRISIS

Billy Connolly used to joke that 'Partick Thistle Nil' is the actual name of the goal-shy Glasgow football club, given how frequently it is heard. In a similar vein, people may assume that 'Police Scotland Crisis' is the national force's official title, given its ubiquity in newspaper headlines.

From the moment it became operational on April Fools' Day 2013 an extraordinary, unprecedented and apparently never-ending tsunami of scandal was unleashed. First came the rogue Counter Corruption Unit (CCU) and its data protection witch-hunt against officers who were fitted up despite often being completely innocent. Rather than rooting out real corruption, the unit was accused of going for the 'low hanging fruit' of data breaches, a catch-all term covering a multitude of misuse in relation to stored records. Reputations, health, families and careers were destroyed, but that was just the beginning of the maelstrom that followed.

There were blunders, bullying and backstabbing, greed and corruption, deaths and dishonesty. The viewing public watched aghast at each shocking episode of this explosive – and very expensive – real-life soap opera. Unlike TV drama, there was no off button. The honest and decent majority of officers could only despair.

The first two chief constables – Sir Stephen House and Phil Gormley – were forced out prematurely. Political meddling by successive SNP justice ministers fuelled fears that policing was becoming a political plaything, moulded to fulfil the nationalist government's agenda. The Scottish Police Authority was supposed to be a public guardian. Instead it bent to the will of the justice ministers. Perhaps worse, it became a cabal of cronies more interested in staging cover-ups, instilling secrecy and grabbing fistfuls of taxpayers' cash than holding the police to account.

To understand why Bill's story did not seem to be treated with the seriousness and urgency that it deserved, it is necessary to set out the quite incredible roll-call of competing scandals.

Father of two Sheku Bayou, 31, died in Kirkcaldy, Fife, while being restrained by officers in May 2015. The police response – instinctive and typical – was secrecy and silence. Demands for answers for Sheku's family were met with an attempt to smear a dead man, compounded with a whiff of racism. At the time of writing, the family still do not know what happened.

That same year, a member of the public reported a car crash on the M9 motorway. The vehicle contained John Yuill, 28, and Lamara Bell, 25. For three days, fatally injured Lamara was trapped beside the lifeless body of John. By the time she was found, it was too late. Not only had police failed to act on the call, they had separately issued a public plea to find the missing couple. Lessons learned? Apparently not.

The following year the body of David Penman was discovered in his van. Over the previous 48 hours the police had received several phone calls about it being parked on a rural Stirlingshire road but failed to respond.

Andrew Bone, 36, was vulnerable and lived alone in Edinburgh. Over a seven-day period police received four separate reports from concerned council officials and members of the public. Two of these were 999 calls, stating that Andrew may have hurt or killed himself. The police ignored them. On the seventh day, they broke down his flat door to find him dead.

In such cases, relatives often voiced 'no faith' in the police, as the initial errors were compounded by disingenuous or dishonest responses. Blunders due to human failings or limited resources are one thing, insidious duplicity is quite another.

The following examples perhaps serve to illustrate something worse than mere incompetence – perhaps institutional failures in which a casual acceptance of dishonesty has somehow become normalised.

When it emerged that gun-toting officers had begun to regularly patrol Scotland's streets, there was an outcry. That the public were not consulted was the greater issue and perhaps illustrative of a new breed of police chief, trained in management speak and detached from the people who fund their six-figure salaries and generous pensions. When journalists uncovered the armed police scandal, senior officers responded with obfuscation and untruths. Not for the last time, MSPs accused senior officers of lying to them in parliament.

It emerged that more people in Scotland were subjected to the controversial tactic of 'stop and search' than in London. They included hundreds of children under the age of 12. A senior officer told a Holyrood committee the 'indefensible' child searches would end. A year later it emerged that 356 children had been targeted since the pledge, leading to fresh accusations of parliament being lied to, further undermining public trust. Somehow, such casual misleading of elected politicians seemed to become acceptable. For the top brass to readily lie further eroded the public trust needed to maintain effective policing.

When a newspaper unmasked a 'forgotten suspect' in the unsolved Emma Caldwell murder, the police turned their attention on how the press had found out about it and the toxic CCU conducted an illegal spying operation in order to identify the source of the embarrassing revelations. Once caught out, evasive and aloof senior officers kept on digging. Three years later the despairing chief constable of an English police force – tasked with investigating the illegal snooping – told MSPs at Holyrood: 'It was very clear to me we were being asked to do an investigation. We were then told "This isn't an investigation, this is an enquiry." That's when I became a little bit confused and a little bit concerned. I think there was a lack of openness in certain parts of the investigation, and remains so. Certainly in the legal department. There isn't any conspiracy in Police Scotland. This is ineptitude. People have dug themselves into the trenches.'

These powerful words, coming from a respected and high-ranking officer, made a mockery of incessant and dismissive background noise from Police Federation officials with a taste for status quo comfort and ex-senior cops with a taste for the limelight. According to them, the press was to blame for daring to look for problems and that only the police were qualified to comment on policing matters. 'Nothing to see here' was the shrill mantra – which became increasingly self-serving and ludicrous as the scandals multiplied.

One former superintendent, a frequent provider of media soundbites, told the BBC: 'What does sap morale is the continual newspaper headlines. It's a topic that everybody thinks they know something about because they've watched *The Bill* or *Z-Cars* when whey grew up and they think they know about policing.' A classic example of shooting the messenger.

These comments may have been directed at Moi Ali, a

quietly determined public servant who speaks out when required, rather than staying mute and taking the easy money while sitting on public boards. Ali quit as Scotland's first Judicial Complaints Reviewer after exposing the post as a toothless watchdog and a pale shadow of the comparable organisation for people in England and Wales who have cause to complain about judges. Ali's stand infuriated the judicial elite and the SNP government. She was later forced to quit the Scottish Police Authority (SPA) board in protest at the imposition of secrecy in which meetings were held in private and agendas were not published in advance. Lost in the initial media reports was the SPA's decision to scrap a subcommittee whose job was to investigate complaints against senior officers. It was a committee that would have had plenty to keep it busy.

Numerous scandals eventually forced out Stephen House, which saw at least one outstanding complaint against him being dropped. Waiting in the wings with an eye on the top job were deputy chief constables Neil Richardson and Iain Livingstone – but they had no chance. Richardson, fluent in jargon, had been tainted by numerous scandals under House's autocratic watch, some of which called into question his honesty.

Livingstone was a former lawyer and good talker who had courted the SNP establishment, had friends in the media but was previously cleared of allegations of sexual assault by a female officer. Livingstone was, however, found guilty of breaching rules by staying overnight at the woman's room at a police venue, but there were serious concerns about his protracted disciplinary process which saw him suspended and demoted four ranks, only for that punishment to be overturned on appeal. That the alleged victim was the subject of a smear campaign in the press was despicable. Post-Harvey Weinstein, there were too many unanswered questions and the opacity of the process did not instil confidence. The case later served to illustrate an often cosy relationship between the policing elite and the political class when Green MSP and ex-police officer John Finnie gently questioned Livingstone at Holyrood – while failing to disclose that he had been his Police Federation rep during the sex assault process.

Another of this imperious elite was deputy chief constable Rose Fitzpatrick, a recruit from London. SPA finance official Amy McDonald questioned why Fitzpatrick had received £18,000 in relocation expenses, then a further £49,000 the following year. Fitzpatrick asked for their chunk of taxpayers' money by bank transfer, rather than through the payroll system, prompting McDonald to later tell an employment tribunal: 'The deputy chief constable asked for a cash transfer, which does not go through the tax system. I could not see any exceptional circumstances to support this payment.'

For reasons known only to the SPA, Fitzpatrick received a further £53,000 to settle her personal tax bill. After bravely challenging the unorthodox spending, the whistleblower said her employers then tried to 'threaten and frighten' her. Ridiculously, they accused her of 'creating a terrorist threat' against Fitzpatrick by including the officer's personal details in internal documents. These had only mentioned Fitzpatrick's town and county, not her actual address or postcode. Audit Scotland, which is supposed to keep track of public spending, criticised the SPA's 'unacceptable' use of public money.

When Police Scotland was two years old, veteran English officer Phil Gormley came out of retirement to take over from Stephen House. Richardson left while defeated Livingstone regrouped. Gormley probably wishes he hadn't bothered. The *Scottish Daily Mail*'s headline 'A No-Nonsense Copper's Cop' perhaps gave a clue to what would follow. An observation in the *Scottish Sun* hinted

at the embarrassing parochial mindset that still pervades
sections of Scottish society: 'The appointment of another
officer from down south has put some noses out of joint.
But who cares if he's English?'

Tasked with restoring public confidence, Gormley
appears to have been doomed from the outset. A whispering campaign began. The 'no-nonsense copper'
was a bully, it was alleged. Less than two years into his
£214,000-a-year tenure, the allegations led to Gormley
offering to step aside on 'special leave' in order that
they be resolved. He never returned. Five months later
he resigned, having still not been spoken to, nor had the
allegations put to him. That the chief's future was not the
SPA's number one priority is bewildering.

The SPA had agreed that Gormley should return to
work but their decision was reversed after an unminuted
meeting with justice minister Michael Matheson, prompting further allegations of political meddling. New bullying
complaints suddenly emerged, prompting accusations
of a stitch-up. CCU victims, crushed by the same system,
knew the feeling.

The public would never learn the details of what was
alleged about Gormley, let alone the truth. The reaction
from respected policing figures was scathing. Sir Hugh
Orde, a former president of the Association of Chief
Police Officers, said, 'If the allegations are as straightforward as bullying, it is extraordinary that the investigation
has taken so long not to reach any conclusion. That cannot be satisfactory for anybody.'

Ali stepped in to demand that the bullying allegations
should be investigated, both for the sake of Gormley and
those who complained.

The chief's wife Claire Gormley, herself a former lead
officer for Her Majesty's Inspectorate of Constabulary in
England and Wales, described the protracted investigation

as a 'disproportionate fishing expedition' tainted with half-truths and a lack of transparency. Being an English 'outsider' may have counted against him. Damningly, she said that she held 'little trust in the institutions charged with investigating and holding Police Scotland to account'.

During a later BBC Radio Scotland discussion show, one former senior detective talked up Livingstone as an 'outstanding' replacement to Gormley and then, perhaps tellingly, felt the need to point out that he was Scottish.

Sergeant Kevin Storey was jailed for nine years in 2014 for raping a woman and sexually assaulting another two. Four years later it emerged that one of his victims, a female colleague, had accused senior officers of suppressing the original criminal complaint against Storey, who happened to be Right Worshipful Master in his local masonic lodge.

When the victim first reported Storey, she claimed she was bullied and forced from her job, later telling journalist Patricia Kane of the Scottish *Mail on Sunday*, 'These senior officers made me feel ashamed to be in the police force. I couldn't believe I was surrounded by such corruption. They did everything they could to break me and make me go away.'

So tainted were Police Scotland, and so slow their apparent investigation into the cover-up allegations, that the Crown Office issued an edict demanding that an independent police force should take over. And still the tide of sleaze rose higher. In early 2018 it was reported that in a period of six months a new unit responsible for internal complaints has received 562 allegations of abuse of authority, theft, fraud and sexual misconduct against police officers.

Scottish policing's squalid civil war – which shows no signs of abating – is a tawdry, selfish and self-indulgent betrayal of communities and crime victims. It also undermines the daily grind of ordinary cops, who continue making a real difference to people's lives in adverse conditions and with shrinking resources. Through overuse, 'Police Scotland Crisis' lost its potency and the public went from shocked to angry, then confused and, finally, numbed by it all.

What is often forgotten is the palpable detriment caused. Immeasurable policing hours continue to be lost to this manmade, cult-like craziness. Against this unedifying backdrop, fighting a rigged system where lies blow in the wind like confetti, what chance of redress and justice for an ordinary member of the public such as Bill?

37

FOOL ME TWICE

Police officers still write statements in long hand. It is slow and painstaking work, which often causes witnesses to ask why, in our digital age, they are not inputted directly into computers. Bill had lost chunks of his life to patiently watching detectives slowly scratch out his spoken words onto paper. Every one of the dozens of reported crimes followed the same inky, time-consuming ritual – speak, pause, write and repeat, concluding with Bill's signature being added to the handwritten pages. There have been dozens of statements about threats, fires, corrosive substances, blades, violence and inadequate investigations. The lengthiest so far, comprising 38 pages, was imparted to Detective Inspector Stevie Watson in June 2013. It was about police corruption. The subsequent dispiriting disappointment of Watson's flaccid report rendered that exercise a waste of time. By late 2017, Bill would sit down yet again in order to impart yet another lengthy account to a yet another detective, pen in hand.

The civil case against Police Scotland had been put on hold on the advice of Bill's lawyer Neil Beardmore, primarily to allow Lcs Brown at the Crown Office's Criminal Allegations Against the Police Division (CAAPD) to consider his allegations of criminality against officers. When, after 15 months, Brown shelved any prosecution 'on the basis of evidence presently available', the civil case was revisited. But Beardmore suggested that before Bill and Jackie committed themselves to a costly, lengthy and risky journey through court, they should give the police one final shove – a last-ditch attempt to force a sincere and thorough criminal inquiry into the fake record and all allegations of police criminality stemming from it. The lawyer further advised that if the police continued to duck and dive – as they anticipated – this could also bolster the civil claim by showing a judge that all efforts at redress had been exhausted before troubling the courts.

Bill wrote to Iain Livingstone, who was standing in as chief constable while Phil Gormley remained on voluntary leave amid allegations of bullying and other crises engulfing policing. This resulted in Bill being contacted by Detective Inspector Clark Hill, who invited him to attend Govan police station, where he offered the assurance that, despite all that had gone before, he was able to be independent in his execution of the enquiry and asked if Bill felt comfortable providing a statement.

Mindful of the saying 'fool me once, shame on you; fool me twice, shame on me', Bill agreed but proceeded with caution and suspicion. He asked who Hill's bosses were. When it was conceded that one of them was DCI Andrew Edward, who he referred to as 'Andy' and whose office was along the corridor, any hopes of an independent inquiry evaporated. With that in mind, Bill still agreed to give the statement to Hill and this took place during half a dozen or so sessions, usually starting around 10 a.m. and finishing by early afternoon.

Hill proceeded to write down what had happened from the moment of John Lawson's alleged threats in April 2009 and the garage fire seven months after that. The police had already conceded failings in many of the CID's investigations during the crime vendetta but Bill explicitly explained why this had not been due to negligence through laziness or incompetence, but wilful neglect, a pattern of criminal behaviour by detectives who were out to bury him, driven by a false belief that he was as a violent, dishonest criminal and troublemaker.

At the heart of it remained Bill's central allegation: that an officer had maliciously created an intelligence system marker resulting in his bogus yet devastating rap sheet.

Bill believed that Hill was sincere in his intent, but as 2017 gave way to 2018 it became evident that indulging another exercise in the police policing themselves would be futile. By the end of January, Bill's testimony had filled around 50 pages of Hill's handwriting, although none had yet been signed. This first tranche related to officers junior to Hill. Bill explained that as they went forward, it was unreasonable to expect Hill to take a statement about alleged criminality by officers of the same and more senior ranks.

As Bill says: 'I anticipated that when it reached the stage of more senior officers being implicated, there would need to be a frank discussion about what should happen next. Up until that point, I had given information alleging criminality by junior officers. I had the details at my fingertips and could back up everything I said, which ought to have shown that I was not some crank making spurious claims. Had that been the case they would not have given me the time of day. In fact, they would have come after me for making false allegations.

'I explained that it would be inappropriate to give a statement to Hill about officers more senior in rank to himself. I did not doubt his professionalism or sincerity but it would put him in an impossible position and I had no faith that my complaints would not disappear into another black hole or the most important parts be ignored, as had happened before. The only remote hope at getting justice would be to remove my case entirely from Police Scotland, or at the very least from the CID. I explained all this to Hill in January 2018, which was our last meeting. He said he would get back to me but I heard nothing further. As expected, that's when the wheels came off.'

In early February, Bill then wrote to Hill, succinctly restating his position about police criminality before laying down what he wanted to happen next. He wrote:

> This saga began in 2009 and it has already taken up far too much of my time, money and effort, not to mention police resources. Over the past nine years the way my complaint has been handled by Strathclyde Police and Police Scotland has been farcical with elements of selectivity, withheld information, dishonesty, glaring conflicts of interest along with other criminality, negligence and misconduct.
>
> On that basis, I have absolutely no faith in Police Scotland, nor the supposedly independent Police Investigations and Review Commissioner, being able to conduct an impartial investigation.
>
> Given the above, I respectfully request that my complaint, and the partial statement I have already provided to you, should be passed to another police force, independent of Police Scotland and PIRC. I believe the seriousness of the criminal allegations, the senior rank of some of those accused, sensitive issues about the integrity of the Scottish Intelligence Database and allegations pertaining to two MSPs [Sandra White and Bill Kidd] are more than enough to justify this course of action.

Hill responded by saying that the case would be sent to the force's Professional Standards Department (PSD) for consideration – plunging it into another abyss and effectively shunning Bill's request for independent, outside scrutiny.

Bill turned to the MSP Professor Adam Tomkins for help. Following a meeting with the Scottish Conservative politician and legal academic, Bill asked him to intervene by echoing his request that only an outside force could conduct a fair investigation and asking them for a proper answer about how the bogus criminal record had been applied.

Bill told the MSP's office: 'I think that a letter from him reiterating my concerns would be helpful and could not so readily be ignored. Furthermore, and central to the entire saga, is my belief that the police's explanation about how I was falsely assigned a criminal record is not credible. While the police may provide a similar answer to Professor Tomkins, perhaps, there may be a way of challenging their explanation.'

Tomkins replied that he had written to a 'very senior officer with whom I have a good professional relationship' and who had responded with the claim that 'an additional review of your most recent complaint is currently being undertaken'.

Bill, well used to chicanery and evasion, was disappointed at the response given to the MSP, telling him: 'I am surprised to learn that the police claim to be conducting "an additional review" of my complaint. This is untrue. Rather, as they know, I have made specific criminal allegations against numerous police officers and this forms the partial statement I have provided to DI Clark Hill. The police's response to you is unfortunate but typical of the dishonesty and obfuscation that has characterised my protracted ordeal in which fairness and due process have been routinely flouted.'

In the intervening weeks, Bill had still heard nothing

from Hill or the PSD, prompting another letter questioning why. He also raised fresh concerns about how a mystery 'very senior' officer appeared to have misled an MSP.

Bill – neither expecting nor receiving a reply – wrote:

> Professor Tomkins was told in writing that the police
> are conducting an 'additional review' of my original
> complaint. This is untrue. As you are aware I have made
> specific criminal allegations against numerous police
> officers, some of which form the partial statement I
> have provided to you. It is of great concern that Police
> Scotland provided false information to an elected
> politician. I would be grateful if you could provide an
> explanation for this.

Yet again, Bill had attempted to honestly engage with the
process in order to get answers. This prompted the usual
soothing reassurances of a speedy and fair investigation,
only to be stymied by reality. The saying that 'insanity is
doing the same thing over and over again, but expecting
different results' did not apply. Bill knew the outcome but,
due to legal advice, he had no choice but to go through
the motions. The police tactic of selectively interpreting
what to consider and using time as a weapon had predict-
ably been deployed. What made this occasion different
was the police's willingness to issue questionable claims
to a politician.

Bill considered turning to the media but it was immersed
in a seemingly never-ending news feed of police oppro-
brium. The chief constable Gormley had just resigned, the
allegations of bullying against him unheard and untested.
BBC Scotland was moved to conduct an investigation into
the force's first five ignominious years, which resulted in
a 30-minute documentary *A Force in Crisis*, containing yet
more toxic revelations. This included an interview with

interim Chief Constable Iain Livingstone, who was asked about past allegations of sexually assaulting a female colleague in her room at a police college in 2000. Livingstone was cleared of criminality but suspended from duty, then demoted from superintendent to constable, for spending the night at the colleague's room. He merely 'fell asleep in the wrong place', having had 'too much to drink', he explained, before adding that his demotion was reversed on appeal.

The longevity and complexity of Bill's case could have filled a mini-series, and by speaking out his voice may have been drowned out by the sheer volume of all the other scandals.

In some respects, while the latest police complaints charade did not help Bill's blood pressure, it was a distraction from the real show – the writ which was lodged in court, primed and ready like a ticking time bomb.

It was at this time that five judges at the Supreme Court delivered their verdict on a case brought against the police in London by victims of the serial 'black cab rapist' John Worboys. They unanimously ruled that people should be able to sue the police for botched investigations.

The Met Police's failure to properly investigate two women's sexual assault allegations against Worboys amounted to inhuman and degrading treatment in breach of the European Convention of Human Rights and trumping the police's defence that imposing such a duty of care on officers would harm operational effectiveness.

As BBC home affairs correspondent Dominic Casciani explained, 'It is not about the compensation, but the duty that the police are now under to carry out an effective investigation – and prove that they have done so. Put most simply, the law has repeatedly made clear that police cannot in general terms be sued for negligence.

'The Supreme Court justices could have limited their

ruling to saying there was only a breach if a force was guilty of systemic failings such as back office bungling because detectives were poorly managed.

'But they went far further – and by a majority ruled that a force had to show that its actual investigation – the specific operational steps taken to hunt down the attacker – were effective.'

It was the verdict that Bill, and Beardmore, had been waiting and hoping for.

38

WAITING TO DIE

When lawyers are asked for an opinion, layers of caveats and qualifications often serve to further confuse clients in need of clarity. Senior Police Scotland officers tasked with giving answers tend to frustrate with jargon, waffle and sleight of hand. Members of the medical profession, however, are more inclined to plain speaking. After all, nuance and ambiguity are of little help to anyone receiving a life-changing diagnosis, as Jackie can affirm. The consultant sat down opposite her and Bill, then gave it to her straight: 'The dark shadows on your lung are cancerous.'

It was a year since the death of Jackie's dad and two years after her mother had passed away. Aged 58, she was too young to die. Further tests revealed the relatively good news that the disease had been caught early and was contained. Just over a fortnight later, in May 2018, she underwent major surgery lasting seven hours. Part of a lung was excised and, with it, hopefully all trace of the dark shadows which had shown up on X-rays like stubbed-out cigarettes.

In the days before going under the surgeon's scalpel, Jackie expressed bitterness towards the police. 'The financial losses we have suffered are obscene,' she said. 'Everything was taken away from us. Late in life we had to virtually start from scratch and will be forced to keep working for longer than we intended. Our retirement plans have been ruined. But even worse is the loss of so much time, which we can never recover. When I was told I had cancer, that became even more real, more painful.'

Jackie, stupefied with morphine in post-op intensive care, was spared from watching Livingstone's TV outing but it, and much else in the programme, added to Bill's conviction that Police Scotland was unwilling, in fact incapable, of investigating its own people.

Other than discovering the chief's apparent narcolepsy, BBC reporter Sam Poling unearthed documents showing how Police Scotland's first boss, Sir Stephen House, softened and attempted to suppress a report containing allegations of serious corruption and criticism of the top brass. The chief's office demanded the removal of negative comments, a section where frontline officers described working in a culture of fear and changing tenses to suggest problems were fixed.

Early drafts included allegations of unauthorised surveillance, threatening and intimidating witnesses, unlawfully detaining suspects, colluding while compiling statements and failing to reveal evidence – all axed from the final version. This flagrant disregard for the integrity of an official report, at the very top of the police, spoke to the same culture that Bill had experienced. As a fish rots from the head, Police Scotland's disregard for truthfulness seems to have percolated downwards. The next day at Holyrood, MSPs debated the latest scandal, with Scottish Conservative justice spokesman Liam Kerr thundering, 'It appears that the head of our national police force has engaged in a deliberate cover-up of allegations of corruption, and changed the tenses of other problems to suggest they were already fixed.'

The BBC revelations added to Bill's incredulity and

contempt. He said: 'Livingstone came across as slippery. From all the years of dealing with this, I cannot believe the low calibre of many senior officers in Police Scotland. He wouldn't have made it to lance bombardier in 16 Regiment. I would have eaten him alive if he had given me answers the way he did on TV.'

Around the same time, Karen Harper, a former police officer with 22 years' service, spoke about her own ordeal at the hands of Police Scotland. After accusing a sergeant of bullying her, Harper was allegedly targeted in a sinister and secret 'black op' to discredit her. Once cleared of any wrongdoing she embarked on a lengthy fight for justice but her eyes were soon opened to the ineffective reality of dealing with PIRC and SPA, deeming them to be a 'firewall' around the police rather than bodies which hold them to account. The whistle-blower summed it up by saying that challenging the police establishment was like taking on the Mafia. Her fight continued, her legal bills rose further from £45,000 and beyond. The cost to her health, happiness and well-being can never be measured.

By the beginning of May 2018, Detective Inspector Clark Hill had still not addressed Bill's request, first expressed three months earlier, to remove the case from Police Scotland's grip and pass it to an outside force. After the withering assessment of Police Scotland by the chief constable of Durham, it was hardly surprising. Nor had there been a response about why an unidentified 'very senior' officer had apparently misled the MSP Professor Adam Tomkins. As for an honest explanation about the criminal record? Still nothing. Those three months of silence added to the years already wasted, but they were more keenly felt due to the devastation wrought by Jackie's lung cancer. Time had never been more precious.

While Bill's lawyers were encouraged by the case brought by victims of rapist Worboys, with the Supreme Court ruling that police did owe a duty of care towards victims, it was no guarantee that his claim would be successful. Taking on a public body with unlimited funds would be to gamble with everything – equivalent to staking their desire for some comfort in their final years on the spin of a roulette wheel. The police complaints system is a rigged game, akin to a mob-run Vegas casino where the house always wins. He viewed the rarefied courts in much the same was as they prioritised the interests of the clubby legal profession over litigants seeking justice. No matter which side wins or loses, the lawyers always get paid. With such high stakes, and with Jackie in need of months of gentle recuperation, some would regard pursuit of justice as a risk not worth taking. Bill and Jackie would have many long conversations about whether to proceed with the legal claim but he remained resolute in his determination for the truth.

'I know that it would destroy him to drop it,' Jackie said. 'He couldn't.'

The secrecy and dishonesty that seems to permeate Police Scotland like a sickness serves no positive purpose but instead generates injustice. Whether members of the public or whistle-blowers, they incur great financial cost, their lives and careers are destroyed. This fuels suspicion of the authorities in an era where that fire needs no additional fuel.

How anyone's identity can be misappropriated by the police – whether mistakenly or maliciously – and be morphed into an alias of a criminal is scandalous. That the integrity of such a sensitive database is not apparently taken seriously by the police should be of concern to anyone. To treat an army veteran with such visceral contempt is contemptuous. Is it likely that Bill is the only person this has happened to?

Just as the police tell us how many crimes have shifted online, altering the traditional landscape of real-world offending, so too that rogue police officers are no longer constrained by face-to-face threats and fit-ups against those considered troublemakers. It seems they too are able to act nefariously in the digital ether.

It is not easy for Jackie to articulate the extent of her personal suffering. 'To be honest, it's difficult to know where to start,' she said. 'Life for us became a living nightmare at the end of 2009. During the ensuing years I lost my job, we had property destroyed, friends stopped contacting me, my mother and one of my sisters disowned me and have never spoken to me since. I came close to taking my own life.

'We received threatening texts and were being stalked. During all of this I was caring for my elderly father who lived with us as he was suffering dementia. My relationship with Bill came under great strain. Then there were the unjust arrests and court cases to deal with.

'Life for us was not "normal". We were under constant strain, alert to being followed, alert to strange people and cars around the house, hiding cars up side streets were habits we would live by for years to come.

'I became increasingly isolated from friends and my health started to deteriorate. I resent all these wasted years taken from us by a madman and aided and abetted by Police Scotland.

'When we discovered that Bill had been given a record we started to understand why we had been treated so badly by so many people. It is disgraceful that after all these years we are still having to fight for answers regarding the record. I always used to have faith in the police . . . that's gone. They changed our lives. They should be ashamed about the way we have been treated.'

Jackie's diagnosis came as a great shock to Bill, who turned 60 in 2017.

'It hit me in a different way,' he said. 'I was even more

angry than Jackie. When my garage burned to the ground I was 52 years old. We have lost almost a decade to this and I believe it contributed to Jackie's ill health. They're waiting for us to give up or die.'

Due to Police Scotland's many scandals in its first five years, MSPs on Holyrood's Justice Committee launched a review of the law that created the national force. Bill, with misgivings about whether it would achieve anything, could not let the opportunity pass, and in August 2018 felt compelled to provide a detailed written submission about his ordeal.

It began: 'Central to my ordeal is Police Scotland's admission that I was assigned an extensive and serious criminal record by the police and my belief that this inaccurate and damaging record meant that my complaints were not investigated properly. I have no criminal convictions. Only due to sustained effort by myself did Police Scotland eventually admit this happened in "error".

'This admission came in the form of a letter from the police in August 2015, stating that the police had "entered your details as being an alias of an existing record holder". However, this explanation is only partial. I believe that it is almost certain that my details were added to a police computer system as an intelligence marker. It is my view that this was not an "error" but a malicious and criminal act by a police officer. The consequences were truly devastating.'

Over three pages, Bill laid out the lurid key details, concluding with a call for an end to the police being able to police themselves and expressing a willingness to give evidence in person to the committee.

Many weeks later he discovered that the committee had decided not to take personal testimony from him or any other individuals, some of whom had also suffered injustice at the hands of the police. The sense of being snubbed was compounded, as the committee clerks failed to inform Bill of the decision, which he only discovered by chance through a third party. It was another door closed. If our elected representatives are uninterested, he thought, what hope for anyone else who may find themselves plunged into a similar abyss of a fake criminal record and a crime vendetta?

While Bill's education in 1970s Easterhouse did not feature Latin, the phrase *Quis custodiet ipsos custodes?* ('Who will guard the guards themselves?') never felt more relevant. In Scotland, it seems the answer remains 'themselves'.

'I learned there is no point in writing to Police Scotland and expecting good faith or an honest answer,' he said. 'PIRC, the SPA and Crown Office are also a waste of time. They are either part of the same police family or have no interest in challenging them in a meaningful way. The police have stolen nearly 10 years of our lives but they get away with it, and will continue, because the politicians and regulators allow them to.'

During the Troubles in Northern Ireland, Bill witnessed a landscape of warring and sometimes hidden factions, who would step out every morning knowing they may never return. He respected the RUC officers on the ground but the management class was a different breed. He sees worrying parallels between the hierarchy of Troubles-era policing in Northern Ireland and today's Police Scotland.

His assessment is bleak and damning and, if nothing else, he deserves the last word.

'There were all sorts of cliques and gangs within the police and military,' he said. 'Many uniformed cops were decent guys doing a very dangerous job but there was an element in Special Branch and the higher ranks who ignored the rules and twisted reality to suit their agenda. Given the environment – where death could be around any corner – it was understandable to some extent.

'I would go as far as saying the culture of Police Scotland, its hierarchy and the CID in particular is worse than what I saw during the Troubles. At least in Northern Ireland, the enemy was trying to kill them, whereas in Scotland the police hierarchy think nothing of treating ordinary, honest and hard-working people like me as the enemy.'